Social Exchange, Dramaturgy and Ethnomethodology

TOWARD A PARADIGMATIC SYNTHESIS

Jack N. Mitchell

Elsevier · New York

NEW YORK · OXFORD

Elsevier North Holland, Inc.
52 Vanderbilt Avenue, New York, New York 10017

Distributors outside the United States and Canada:

Thomond Books
(A Division of Elsevier/North Holland Scientific Publishers, Ltd)
P.O. Box 85
Limerick, Ireland

Library of Congress Cataloging in Publication Data

Mitchell, Jack N
  Social exchange, dramaturgy and ethnomethodology:
toward a paradigmatic synthesis

  Includes bibliographical references and index.
  1. Social exchange. 2. Drama—Technique.
3. Sociology—Methodology. I. Title.
HM73.M57   301'.01   78-13198
ISBN 0-444-99057-7

Manufactured in the United States of America

Designed by Loretta Li

For Deena, Cathy, Ali and Jess

Contents

Preface

This work seeks to develop a new synthesis of sociological theory. It deals specifically with three unique strains of theorizing: social exchange, dramaturgy and ethnomethodology. The format for the argument involves a critical and historiographic analysis of the works of key figures in each of these subdisciplines. Through the identification and analysis of substantive areas of deficiencies and limitations of each, along with notable and unique contributions from each, a chorus is formed from previously separate and incomplete voices.

Scholarship of this sort is most often a solitary enterprise. The present effort however was aided by the numerous suggestions and contributions of others. Stanford Lyman's own writings and the help and encouragement he offered with mine were invaluable assets. Similarly, Arthur Vidich will find much in this work that has benefited from his aid and assistance. Their suggestions, along with those of Marnia Lazreg, are implicit throughout the manuscript.

We are in many ways products of our teachers. I have been

fortunate to have had many very good ones; among these the particular excellences of Peter Berger and Deborah Offenbacher figured most formatively in the development of my own sociological imagination.

A unique and very special debt is owed to my wife, Deena, and my children (Catherine, Alexandra and Jessica). Books are often demanding of time and energies which must, of necessity, be extracted from other times and places. I am fortunate to have a very patient and understanding family—for this I am in debt to them.

Finally, I extend my appreciation to William Gum at Elsevier, for his tireless efforts and editorial assistance.

While this work displays contributions from among a wide range of instructional and intellectual precursors I, of course, take full responsibility for whatever errors or limitations it contains.

O N E : : *Introduction*

INTRODUCTION

This is a study of sociological theory. In its broadest application it deals with various attempted solutions to the basic Hobbesian "problem" of the source and maintenance of order. More directly it attempts to identify and offer correctives for limitations of one sociological answer to this broader question—that of social exchange theory.

With origins in economics, anthropology and psychology in addition to those from classical sociological thought, the tenets of social exchange have emerged as a major arena for the development of sociological theory. Its advocates variously offer it as a corrective for deficiencies of other sociological perspectives and as the central and underlying explanation for the processes and forms of all social behavior. The tenets of social exchange theory have also been instrumental in the development of more specific operationalized schemata for behavioral analysis, such as game theory.

As with any theoretical perspective which enjoys considerable popularity, social exchange has been expanded and elaborated into a number of variants. However, whether they take the form of a general treatise, an attempt to develop law-like propositions or a concrete operationalized motif, all current theories of social exchange would appear to be premised upon similar if not identical renditions of proposed general properties of social interaction. In their broadest possible form these properties are subsumed under Simmel's suggestion that "all contacts among men rest on the schema of giving and returning the equivalence."[1] Different theoretical and operationalizing ventures have embellished this concept to levels where they would appear to be reflective of different, if not opposing, things. Most often, however, the discerning and distilling observer will be able to identify common conceptual groundwork.

It follows, then, from this suggestion of common groundwork that the basics of social exchange theory will be best identified when depicted in their most elementary forms. The present study suggests that the writings of George C. Homans and Peter M. Blau best represent these forms. Homans' work is responsible for both initiating social exchange theory into modern sociology and, along with that of Blau, for giving it its "benchmark" conceptualization. All modern developments within this perspective can be measured and assessed relative to the extent of Homans' and Blau's own theoretical and operationalizing work.

The central thesis of the present study is that social exchange theory (here depicted through Homans' and Blau's writings), for all its apparent appeal as a theory of social behavior claiming to reflect the "basic" properties of such behavior, is wrought with crucial epistemological, theoretical and methodological problems. Central among these are: (1) the tacit, yet sometimes explicit, assumption that human social behavior can thoroughly and accurately be portrayed as following along lines of the non-problematic and rational working out of properties of assumed biological/psychological/economic tendencies; and (2) that structural, institutional properties of society can be traced in their emergence as quantitatively and qualitatively more complex forms of these rational processes. Moreover, it is suggested that these problems with social exchange theory deny it the possibility, in its present form, of ever becoming the comprehensive theory of human social behavior that it often is claimed to be. It is suggested, however, that these problems are resolvable by utilizing correctives to be found outside the conventional and parochial confines of social exchange theory itself. Specifically, these correctives are sought in the particular forms of sociological analyses done under the banners of dramaturgy and ethnomethodology.

The elaborations of these arguments are perhaps best introduced by referring to the specific plan of the present work.

The second chapter deals with Homans' exchange theory. It is suggested that this theory contains a number of crucial problems and limitations which, in one respect, restrict its possible scope of usefulness to a simple two-person direct exchange; and, in another sense, promote an unrealistic view of human social behavior as responsive to an unproblematic rationality of the working out of drives and needs with biological and psychological origins. Homans' difficulties are seen to derive from a number of situational and circumstantial factors. Among these is the unique and eclectic amalgam of sources and derivations of specific conceptions Homans later incorporates into his theory. Homans' training at Harvard is depicted as the arena for this formative mixture.

Also implicated in the sources of difficulties with Homans' theory is his insistence on strict adherence to a particular and limiting theoretical strategy—specifically, explanation from deduction. Homans intends his theory to be nothing less than a reduction-to-cause. The necessity of adhering to the rigor of a deductive system that seeks the origins of social behavior compels Homans to accept, as given and unproblematic, certain aspects of society that would better be derived as emergent forms. The result of this inadequacy at depicting emergence is seen to be a considerable weakness of the theory's ability at handling complex structural properties such as institutions, authority, power, domination and stratification.

In the end, Homans is shown to have attempted to depict the elementary dynamics of exchange relations. However, since the restrictions of his two-person exchange yield a sterile arena for the elaboration of other more complex societal forms, Homans has not produced a comprehensive theory of social behavior; this is because he fails at satisfactorily tracing the evolution of relatively stable structures from the elementary properties of interaction.

Chapter Three concentrates on the work of contemporary sociology's second major exchange theorist, Peter M. Blau. Blau's work is, in large part, an attempt to fill in the void that he sees to exist between reductionist sociologies, such as Homans', and systems sociology, such as Parsons'. While one group is unable to extend its analysis beyond the immediacy of face-to-face exchanges, the other is depicted as unable to reduce its analysis to the real world of everyday behavior. Blau's intent is to bridge this gap and produce a theoretical design that will suggest some form of reduction to basic, emergent properties of social behavior, yet will still be capable of deriving the more complex from these simpler processes.

This program is pursued by first discarding Homans' dependence on operant conditioning as an analytical schema for bringing out the particular human psychology that Homans sees as basic to social behavior; then, by substituting an equally reductionistic economics. This new plan begins with the assumed rationality of motives of self-interest and builds upon a non-problematic working out of properties of supply and demand, marginal utility and the like. Blau then links the formative and elementary qualities of self-interest with larger, structural manifestations by means of what amounts to the major contribution of his exchange theory. That is, that social exchange often, and inevitably, is characterized by a structural asymmetry whereby "returning the equivalence" is unobtainable by some. In many of these instances it is suggested that the result is a natural emergence of power of some over others. The jump from emergent power to larger structural forms is then depicted as dependent on how power-wielded is seen by those subject to it. With the aid of a previously developed standard for judgment, power is seen as fairly and rightfully applied—or it is seen as illegitimate and unfair. These different perspectives then yield various forms and degrees of institution-alized acceptance processes and opposition processes—all of which are to be viewed insofar as they reflect the structural complexities inherent in larger social units.

Overall, Blau's exchange theory is depicted as a model correc-tive of some difficulties identified in that of Homans. By begin-ning with a different form of reduction-to-cause, that is, the tenets of economic interests, Blau has produced a model that yields some sense of the emergence of institutionalized structures; and he has managed a more realistic view of conflict and conflict processes in human affairs.

Yet, Blau's pre-theoretical statement suffers from many of the same deficiencies depicted in Homans' model. By writing in his own non-problematics in the sense of assumed rationalities of self-interest and economic properties, Blau is seen to produce a non-realistic version of human social behavior. The essentials of his argument are themselves seen as non-realistic in that they are often juxtaposed so as to align mutually exclusive properties. For example, Spencerian self-interest is posited as coexisting with a Durkheimian social morality. In the end, Blau's deficiencies are suggested as consequences of his eclectic and loose theoretical underpinnings. In an attempt to satisfy many, he has violated essential properties of each.

Homans' and Blau's failures at developing a comprehensive theory that is both methodologically and epistemologically accu-rate is shown to be partly a consequence of their omission of a sense of the non-rational, non-assured aspects of social behavior. The elements of pursuit, attempt, failure, negotiation, proble-matics and "processual" uncertainties are claimed to be missing.

5

This omission is dealt with in Chapter Four where the dramaturgy of Erving Goffman is utilized as a corrective that contributes a sense of reality to theories of exchange behavior.

Goffman's dramaturgy, depicted as deriving primarily from groundwork laid by Kenneth Burke, Gustav Ichheiser, George Herbert Mead and Emile Durkheim, is seen to be a useful and necessary corrective to exchange theory. By emphasizing the dramatic, put-on quality of social life, Goffman has portrayed its uncertainties and problematics, and has also depicted the constant and necessary attempts by actors to shore-up structures of interaction and self which are built upon the perpetual jeopardy of actors' existential condition. Goffman's skills at identifying the real-life contingencies of interaction lead us into an appreciation of the need for mutually supportive conspiracies of exchange. These exchanges, taking such structured forms as team performance, ritualization, expression and impression games, allow the individual actor a degree of security and a sense of continuity in an otherwise insecure and disjointed social environment. Men are depicted as tending to conspire to exchange with each other such forgivings and supports as are necessary to maintain the sanctity and continuity of the situation. For it is from the quality of the situation and their successes and failures in it that actors are seen to derive and preserve a sense of identity and self.

For whatever it may contribute to the development of a more comprehensive exchange theory, the use of Goffman's dramaturgy does not solve all the difficulties and, in fact, seems to create some of its own. Goffman's sociology is portrayed as consisting of two essential, separate developments; one is a skillful unearthing of the dynamic and structural details of the phenomenology of everyday behavior; the other is an analysis of the confrontation between the actor and the structural and institutional aspects of society. While the first of these essentials is completely and thoroughly developed, the second is seen to suffer both incompleteness and particularistic "boundedness." This boundedness is pictured as imposed by Goffman's restricting institutional analysis to contingencies of structure *only* as they are context for action.

Goffman is, thus, pictured as lacking a perspective that allows for the development of the general, universal, invariant properties any comprehensive theory of social behavior must obtain.

Chapter Five is the last of the essentials of the argument. Here, through an examination of the ethnomethodological concerns of Harold Garfinkel, a search is made for those invariants of social behavior that may be said to exist. With the recognition that contexts, situations, cultures—the external parameters of inter-action—are subject to change, the search for invariants is done *within* the frame of interaction itself. It is suggested that such internal characteristics are to be seen as phenomena in them-selves.

Through Garfinkel's unique emphasis on the bases for com-mon understanding, derivable from an "inner" course of in-terpretive work (as opposed to such "outer" constructs as insti-tutions, norms, needs, motives, interests, and biographies), the *creative* processes of an exchange of communication are identified and promoted as universal and invariant properties of social behavior. Those meanings and senses of reality that are taken to be inherent in or imposed upon activity are seen to be both constituted *by* and, reflexively, constitutive *of* action itself. By "bracketing" talk and interactive processes Garfinkel demon-strates the existence of a body of tacit knowledge that, in the end, exists as a meaning-endowing invariant structure.

With this statement of invariance, then, the groundwork for the development of a comprehensive portrayal of the essential exchange processes is completed. It remains for the concluding chapter to reconstruct the logic of the preceding argument as a resolution of that which has here, and will throughout, be noted as problems with social exchange theory.

In the conclusion, an attempt is made to draw together various problems with exchange theory and solutions to these problems brought out previously. Ideally, the use of all the threads will promote the weaving of a flawless fabric of resolution and syn-thesis. While this would certainly be desirable, it may not be possible, as a total integration is, perhaps, unrealistic at this time.

However, there are certain thematic developments suggested throughout this work that are presented in the conclusion as resolutions of the deficiencies with exchange theory.

First among these developing themes is the issue of exchange theory's defects in its attempts at a comprehensive statement of human behavior such that all phases and levels of this behavior (e.g., both the interpersonal *and* the institutional) are accounted for. It is suggested that Homans and Blau attempt such a statement, yet both fall short. Goffman's institutional analysis is offered as a corrective for much of exchange theory's failure; yet his work, too, is thought to be limited. For, while he begins to explore the institutional aspects of the stage of human drama he neither completes this analysis nor does he integrate it with his portrayals of the nuances of the actor's trade. What is required is a better depiction and understanding of the institutional settings for exchange behavior. The conclusion attempts this.

The second theme developed here deals with the defects in exchange theory that promote an overly mechanistic portrayal of human social behavior. Beginnings in areas such as human and animal biology, reductionist psychology and reductionist economics are seen to lead exchange theorists (Homans and Blau) to depict man as driven by assumed rationalities of need, reward and profit. The conclusion restates the needed corrective that Goffman's portrait of the problematics of human life contributes. It is suggested that mechanistic rationalities are far too simplistic and rigid to promote a real understanding of human behavior. Again, however, Goffman's contribution is not complete. While he produces a detailed, thorough depiction of the problematics and irrationalities of social life, he does not tie this discussion to his otherwise incomplete institutional analysis. My conclusion attempts to remedy the problems this incompleteness leaves unresolved.

The final, major theme dealt with in this work is a natural consequence of the deficiencies noted in the elaboration of the two previous themes—that is, exchange theory, failing as it does with dealing with various levels of human social behavior in a comprehensive way, also fails at depicting whatever universal and invariant properties there may be to such behavior. As a corrective to this deficiency we promote the ethnomethodological studies of Garfinkel. These studies are seen to provide both the focus *within* the interactive frame and the tools with which to search for and identify universals and invariants. The conclusion puts closure to this particular thematic development and integrates it with the others.

The program then, for the conclusion includes first, a critical summary of the issues and arguments raised throughout the work and an attempt at resolution and integration. In the latter effort we introduce the social exchange views of Marcel Mauss.[2] It is suggested that Mauss' writings on exchange behavior in archaic societies provide the catalyst that will enable an integration of the various threads of the arguments here, and a resolution of the problems and issues raised. Mauss will be portrayed as suggesting common ground on which a humanistic social exchange theory will allow for a non-mechanistic view of man, coexisting with a structural, institutional theory of social exchange. Furthermore, it will be suggested that Mauss provides for a determination of the general parameters within which a statement of universal and invariant properties of social behavior can be made.

The conclusion promotes an emergent thesis of social exchange that is suggested as being closer to a comprehensive theory than any previous attempt.

NOTES

1. Georg Simmel, *The Sociology of Georg Simmel*, trans. and ed. Kurt H. Wolff (New York: Free Press, 1950), p. 387.
2. Marcel Mauss, *The Gift: Forms and Functions of Exchange in Archaic Societies*, trans. Ian Cunnison (Glencoe, Ill.: The Free Press, 1954).

T W O : : *A Theory of Social Exchange : George C. Homans*

INTRODUCTION

Like many sociologists before and after him, George C. Homans is generally concerned with contributing to a scientific theory of human social behavior that has the capability of generating universal properties or laws. Homans is, perhaps more than many others, quite specific about how this theory should be constructed and what form it should take when completed. Basically, Homans argues for a theory that *will explain* rather than merely account for phenomena; and, by explanation, Homans specifically refers to a deductive program that includes specific supportable propositions linked in causal chains. The substance of this theoretical program is to include statements about men as men, for only in this fashion, claims Homans, can we identify behaviors and properties of the most universal and elementary nature. The culmination of these intents is the initiation into modern sociology of social exchange theory. The development of contemporary variants of social exchange theory is due primarily to the formulations of this approach in Homans' works. Beginning with a ground-laying statement in 1958,[1] Homans has developed and expanded his brand of exchange theory to the point where it has reached some level of sophistication in his own work, and it has inspired numerous extensions, revisions and commentaries from others.

In this chapter, I intend to trace the development of Homans' scheme from its emergence in his early training as a sociologist through a confrontation with the work of several European and American scholars and into its full development as a theory of social behavior with a uniquely eclectic nature. What should emerge will be a portrait of the intellectual continuity of a particular line of thought as it grows and develops in the work of one man.

In addition to this attempt at an historiographic sketch, I propose to confront Homans' claim of explanation. While I am in general agreement with the exchange model of human behavior, I will suggest that Homans' variant of this theory has several problems that, in the first place, make its deductive underpinnings somewhat weakened and which, secondly, limit its extension to levels more realistically representative of human social behavior.

HOMANS' SOCIAL EXCHANGE THEORY

Sources

Different analysts give vastly differing answers to the question of the origin of Homans' social exchange theory. Mulkay,[2] for example, attributes Homans' direction to an argument with Parsons' brand of functionalism. More recently, Ekeh[3] suggests that Homans' polemics are more with European scholars. He attributes Homans' support of an individualistic social exchange theory to his dissatisfaction with Lévi-Strauss' collectivist doctrine of exchange via cross-cousin marriage.[4] Homans himself is not much help; at times he is certainly enmeshed in a debate with American functionalism,[5] while in other instances he claims to be building on the supposed deficiencies of earlier Europeans—Durkheim, for example.[6] Finally, as if to completely confuse the issue, Homans[7] claims that his social exchange theory is the natural development from his attempt to correct limitations in his earlier descriptive study, *The Human Group*.[8] In fact, while none of these claims is incorrect, none, including that of Homans himself, is complete enough to accurately portray the intellectual and conceptual development of one of contemporary sociology's major theoretical strains.

Homans' interests and motives in offering his contribution to social exchange theory are traceable to a number of sources. An attempt to list them in bio-chronological order would perhaps appear as follows: (1) Homans' early sociological training at Harvard where he absorbed several strains of social thought (primarily those of Pareto, Henderson and Murray),[9] and where he began a career-long orientation to a particular theoretical strategy (induction leading to deduction); (2) Homans' on-going polemic with Durkheimian functionalism and, his related rejection of Comte and a collectivist doctrine; (3) a challenge to certain developments in cultural anthropology (notably the anthropological variant of functionalism); (4) a search for an individualistic theory of social behavior that put him onto psychological behaviorism and utilitarian economics.

I will examine in some detail several of these interests and motives and attempt to support the view that Homans' social exchange theory displays an intellectual continuity throughout its development.

THE EARLY YEARS AT HARVARD. In 1932, fresh from Harvard College where he had concentrated his interests in English literature, Homans found that his form of training did not prepare him for the joblessness of the depression era. Finding himself unemployed, he returned to Harvard to take part in a seminar on the *Sociologie Generale* of the Italian economist, Vilfredo Pareto. The seminar was offered by a professor of biological chemistry, Lawrence Joseph Henderson. The seemingly strange combination of a physiologist conducting a seminar on the work of a social economist is partly understandable when one considers that Pareto was first an engineer and later a sociologist who attempted to incorporate the philosphy and techniques of the natural sciences into a theory of society.

Homans was deeply influenced both by Pareto and Henderson. Of the former Homans notes, "He made clear to me what I was already prepared to believe."[10] The latter Homans honors in the Preface of his introduction to Pareto's sociology in 1934. Since Henderson's intellectual relationship with Homans was in large measure tied to Pareto's thought (both through Henderson's seminar and his own 1935 volume on Pareto), we can treat these two influences together.

The influence of Paretian sociology on Homans was multiple. First, Pareto's work provided Homans with an interest in sociology as a "generalizing science" as opposed to one that would act as an "agency of change or a means of understanding my immediate environment."[11] This early orientation is perhaps to be seen as the foundation of Homans' career-long search for laws of the most universal and general nature regarding human social behavior. Certainly Homans found favor with Pareto's outline for sociology.

> Social facts are the elements of our study. Our first effort will be to classify them for the purpose of obtaining the one and only objective we have in view; the discovery, namely of uniformities (laws) in the relations between them. When we have so classified kindred facts, a certain number of uniformities will come to the surface by induction; and after going a good distance along that primarily inductive path, we shall turn to another, where more room will be found for deduction. So we shall verify the uniformities to which induction has carried us, give them a less empirical, more theoretical form, and see just what their implications are, just what picture they give of society.[12]

In short, Pareto's program for science was to classify a wide range of observable data and to search for uniformity and regularity among them, thus inductively producing a parcel of lawlike propositions from which one might deduce a broader theoretical statement. Pareto chose as models of the successful application of this scientific method the disciplines of astronomy and mechanics (physics).

Homans' own program for sociology is virtually identical to the Paretian formula. Homans calls for a science whose underpinnings are classifications of observable data that are then molded into propositions that, when linked with other propositions, form a causal chain that in its more completed fashion provides for explanation and theory. As one of several prominent sociologists who in the late 1950s and early 1960s voiced opposition to the method inherent in structural-functionalism, Homans specifically objected that functionalists were not constructing legitimate theory—rather, they were dealing in illegitimate teleology, attempting to "explain" problematic societal phenomena by their ultimate *effects* rather than deductively leading up to them by unearthing causes. In his now classic Presidential Address to the American Sociological Association entitled, "Bringing Men Back In,"[13] Homans describes his visions of explanation, theory and, by inference, his vision of the task of sociology:

> An explanation is a theory, and it takes the form of a deductive system.[14]
>
> A theory of a phenomenon consists of a series of propositions, each stating a relationship between properties of nature ... if there is some change in one of the properties, it must at least begin to specify what the change in the other property will be. If one of the properties is absent, the other will also be absent; or if one of the properties increases in value, the other will too.[15]

It is evident that Homans seeks theory that will "explain" by deducing from "properties of nature"—that is, precise empirical data. Homans' work seems singularly devoted to the pursuit of identifiable empirical realities from which he might derive a series of generalizations regarding the nature of human interaction.

14

Certainly this theoretical strategy is not unique with either Pareto or Homans. In fact, one might argue that Homans could have adopted his version from any of a number of sources other than Pareto. However, if we note that Homans was, in effect, ignorant of formal sociology in any of its forms until he read Pareto our claim that this is the source of his theoretical strategy seems to be strengthened.[16]

A second influence, gotten from Paretian sociology, was the recognition of a less-than-logical element in human behavior. In his early work, *An Introduction to Pareto: His Sociology*,[17] Homans notes:

> No sociologist or historian has furnished any intellectual scheme, however crude, which can be applied widely as a tool for the analysis of the politics of the present day. The trouble may perhaps be that when the social scientists have gone about constructing such schemes, since they are themselves trained in logical thinking, they have unconsciously assumed that men in general act logically, and therefore their schemes have been found irrelevant. For few of the important phenomena of recent history can be seen as the result of logical actions. The response to the various Fascisms, Communisms, and Socialisms, to the national government in England, to the New Deal in the United States, are obviously none of them logical, but rather unreasoned and emotional. And this sort of response is the controlling factor in all history, ancient and modern.[18]

> The historians and social scientists, then, have failed to describe recent happenings in any important way, because they have been unable to set up any broad theory of the non-logical actions of men, the most important element determining the form of society.[19]

Again, we note Homans' continuing concern for sociology that *would* explain social phenomena. Homans' indictment of previous efforts centers on their inability to explain the *why* of human behavior because of their overdependence on explanations that involve an assumed logic in man. What Homans sensed at this stage of his development as a sociologist was the need to deal with human beings as less than rational—less than logical beings.

In Pareto, Homans found his theory of non-logical actions. It included: "residues," the manifestations of sentiments; "derivations," the justifications, rationalizations in words for sentiments; and, "interests," or appetites, tastes and impulses. This scheme serves as one source of what Homans later adopts as "sentiments," and much of what he later assumes as "givens"—that is, a *psychological need structure*. We will later turn to a more detailed consideration of this important element.

Another notable figure in Homans' early training was the humanistic psychologist, Henry A. Murray. While there is no evidence from Homans' autobiographical statements of any direct contact with Murray, he was at Harvard before and during Homans' tenure there and apparently had a considerable influence on a wide variety of disciplines, faculty and students.[20] Hall and Lindzey note, "not only did Murray create a sense of excitement and imminent discovery among his own students but also the clinic opened its doors to mature scholars from a variety of fields . . . so that there was a marked interdisciplinary aura to the enterprise."[21] Maddi and Costa suggest that Murray "influenced an entire field and several generations of personologists."[22]

It seems likely that Murray's tenure at Harvard and his diffusion of ideas served to pollinate some of Homans' earlier readings of Pareto. Specifically, Murray's psychology is supportive of two elements basic to similarities in the work of Pareto and Homans. They are Murray's belief that a person avoids pain and pursues pleasure (what one commentary terms a "hedonic calculus,"[23]) and his work on the concept of "needs."

Pareto reflects the hedonic calculus in his elaboration of "interests." For him an interest is an "impulse [which is] spurred by instinct and reason to acquire possession of material goods that are useful—or merely pleasurable—for purposes of living as well as to seek consideration and honours. Such impulses, which may be called 'interests' play in the mass a very important part in determining social equilibrium."[24] Homans incorporates the synthesis of Pareto's conceptualization of interests and the hedonic calculus of Murray into his exchange theory as propositions relating to the probability of repeating acts that have been rewarding in the past.

The second aspect of Murray's psychology that seems to be most amenable to a comparison with Pareto's and Homans' work is the concept of "needs." Perhaps Murray's own words will best describe what he means by this construct. A "need," he writes, is

a construct (a convenient fiction or hypothetical concept) which stands for a force . . . which organizes perception, apperception, intellection, conation and action in such a way as to transform in a certain direction an existing, unsatisfying situation. A need is sometimes provoked directly by internal processes of a certain kind . . . but, more frequently by the occurrence of one of a few commonly effective press . . . thus it manifests itself by leading the organism to search for or to avoid encountering, or, when encountered, to attend and respond to certain kinds of press. [It] gives rise to a certain course of overt behaviour . . . which (if the organism is competent and external opposition not insurmountable) changes the initiating circumstances in such a way as to bring about an end situation which stills (appeases or satisfies) the organism.[25]

Murray continues with an important distinction:

Needs may be conveniently divided into: 1. primary (viscerogenic) needs, and 2. secondary (psychogenic) needs . . . speaking loosely, we may say that from a subjective standpoint the viscerogenic needs have to do with physical satisfactions and the psychogenic needs with mental or emotional satisfactions . . . .[26]

The psychogenic needs are presumably dependent upon and derived from the primary needs . . . .[27] [However;] . . . It is not supposed that they are fundamental, biological drives, though some may be innate.[28]

Of primary interest here is Murray's separation of needs into two types, physical and mental (or emotional) and his assumption that the latter are "dependent upon and derived from" the former. Murray is suggesting that man's emotional and affective need make-up (including such items as the needs for "recognition," "dominance" and "aggression")[29] derives from the satisfaction of primary physical needs. We might note that Murray's classification of need structures is quite similar to the interpretation that Homans gives to Pareto's concept of "residue." A residue for Pareto meant a manifestation of some underlying state of mind, or sentiment. Homans notes:

> The residues fall into two different groups. One is made up of satisfactions of human impulses so fundamental that they might be called biological . . . The second group is made up of the attitudes, habits, uniform and recognized ways of acting, which an organized society imposes on its members, largely by means of their mothers and fathers, who teach them while they are children what is "done" and what is "not done."[30]

What is important here is Homans' distinction between, on one hand, biological (or primary) residues, and on the other, attitudes, habits and a class of more cognitive residues. Later in his development of exchange theory Homans will dwell almost exclusively on rewards of the second class of residues—that is, he will deal with approval, recognition, acceptance and the like. It is important to note that a feasible interpretation of the line of development of these concepts in Homans' work is the derivation of psychological from physical needs in Murray and the distinction Homans finds in Pareto between those expressions of sentiment that are "innate" and those which are "learned." When we examine the concept of need inherent in Homans' work we will return to this interpretation.

THE MIDDLE YEARS. There are several sources for Homans' exchange theory that are considerably different from what we have just examined. For the most part these fall into a chronological and intellectual middle period that reaches beyond the early work on Pareto and stops short of Homans' formal exchange theory of the late 1950s and early 1960s.

Among these sources is the influence of utilitarian economics.

Utilitarianism, a doctrine that in classical sociology is best represented by the work of Herbert Spencer,[31] stresses that individuals'
wants and desires are central to their behavior. In its classical
formulation (e.g., Adam Smith and Jeremy Bentham), man is
portrayed as a rational, deliberative seeker of maximum utility—
or profit; a view that is generalized into broader statements of
equilibrium or of ethics. Early sociologists (e.g., Comte and Durkheim) claimed to recognize the inadequacies of such suggestions,
while man is perhaps "calculating" pay-off e.g., potentials he may
not always be rational; also, it may not be desirable "societally" to
seek maximization of profit. Having pointed out such types of
limitations in utilitarianism, these sociologists sought other bases
for positing the maintenance of societal stability. Comte saw
promise in a collectivist ethic that rode on the crest of developing
positivistic sciences—a religion of positivism that was to save the
world. Durkheim found his solution in the perpetuity of a generalized moral code that stressed the interests of society and the
state over the individualistic calculations of its members.

The derivation of Homans' social exchange theory is also de-
Homans has returned full-tilt to Spencerian utilitarianism (albeit, with a more tenable variant) and denounces the sociologies
of those who would see more in society than merely the sum of
its parts. For example, he rejects Durkheim "as having no final
truth" and Durkheim's assertion that society was an entity *sui
generis* (i.e., that sociology was not a "corollary of psychology")[32]
The "psychology" that Homans has in mind is one which is very
much at home with tenets that are basic to utilitarianism (e.g.,
man, the seeker of profit maximization and cost minimization).
Society's stability, when it appears, is not, for Homans, a result of
a generalized moral code but is the result of a kind of equilibrium
of interest satisfaction, a conceptualization drawn directly from
utilitarianism.[33]

The derivation of Homans' social exchange theory is also dependent on Homans' reading of cultural anthropologists. In
1955, Homans and Schneider published a sixty-four-page book,
*Marriage, Authority, and Final Causes: A Study in Unilateral Cross-
Cousin Marriage.* In this brief work, Homans and Schneider take

issue with the work of the French anthropologist, Claude Lévi-Strauss. Many of their original arguments with Lévi-Strauss have been expanded and repeated in subsequent works by Homans. It is, therefore, important to investigate these origins.

In *Les Structures Elementaire de la Parente*, Lévi-Strauss attempted to explore the rules of marriage patterning in primitive societies (specifically, rules governing cross-cousin marriage). His research concluded that different types of cross-cousin marriage (matrilateral or patrilateral) in different situations foster social solidarity by "generalizing" the rules of marriage (e.g., the exchange of women) into a state of solidarity. Lévi-Strauss suggests a basic tenet of structural-functionalism—that is, the structures and functions which best contribute to the survival of the system tend to persist. Hence, he implies we can "understand" the existence of certain phenomena (marriage patterns) by examining the "effects" they produce (they "work" to maintain solidarity).

Homans and Schneider challenge Lévi-Strauss on epistemological grounds and in terms of the conclusions he reached. First, and foremost, they maintain that Lévi-Strauss's conceptualization of "generalized exchange," as leading to "organic solidarity," is methodologically unacceptable. It is both untestable and reflects an illegitimate teleology. By seeking demonstrations of "effect" in support of arguments, Lévi-Strauss, it is maintained, has short-circuited the process of explanation. Explanation should always be done by "causes"—not by "effects."

Homans and Schneider suggest that the existence of one form or another of cross-cousin marriage is to be explained by reducing the argument to individual psychology, e.g., certain types of matrimonial ties (those into chains constituting the family "locus of jural authority")[34] are discouraging of affection, while others (into chains constitutive of minimal or no authority) are conducive to ties of liking. The result, Homans maintains, is that cross-cousin marriage will follow in the direction of the greatest potential for affective ties between people—for a reason which is basic to Homans' developing psychological reductionism—affective ties are rewarding and people seek that which is rewarding. Rather than the functionalism of Levi-Strauss, Homans, in the end, prefers an "individual self-interest theory" to explain the "survival" of institutional forms:

An institution is what it is because it results from the drives, or meets the immediate needs, of individuals or subgroups within a society. We may call this individual self-interest theory, if we remember that interests may be other than economic.[35]

The next stage in Homans' work is the search for specific statements which will reflect those empirical generalizations he feels are descriptive of the nature of human interaction. In the *Human Group,* published in 1950, Homans examines five detailed studies of human groups (primarily small ones) to develop propositions that relate to classes of variables of human behavior. He identifies four categories that perform as variables in his propositional statements; they are: activity (behavior); sentiment (behavior linked to attitudes); interaction (behavior reflexively linked with responses from others); and norms (situational properties of behavior in statement form). From these classes of variables, Homans produces a number of generalizations of human behavior in propositional form. For example: "the more frequently persons interact with one another, the stronger their sentiments of friendship for one another are apt to be."[36] While this study has resulted in the production of a number of such propositions, Homans himself soon recognized the limitations of this type of broad generalization and sought greater precision in detailing the sort of principles he believed underlie all human social behavior. What he sought were "laws" of fixed and unchangeable properties such that they would "explain" the "why" of human behavior and not merely describe the "what." Ultimately this search led Homans to behavioral psychology, specifically that of B. F. Skinner.[37] In Skinner's work Homans found a series of underlying psychological principles dealing with reward and punishment which seemed to provide the lowest level of reduction-to-cause. This jump to behavioral psychology was already hinted at in *The Human Group.*

For example, Homans' description of the manner in which the group norms of the Bank Wiring Room acted to constrain Taylor's behavior was, in a way, just steps ahead of a behavioral model.

> Taylor came closest to realizing the output standard of the group. He also had the highest social rank, received most interactions from other men . . . and was the most influential member of the group. Any long-continued departure in his activity rate from the norm of the group would have brought about a decline in all of these other things. *So far as he enjoyed his social rank, his associations, and his influence, a change in his output rate would have hurt him. In the relation of each of these elements to all the others in a system lies the fact of control.*[38]

Homans, then, seems to have found a format in which he could deal with his conception of the non-logical aspects of human behavior, and reduce the level of explanation to properties *basic* enough to be *explanatory*. Skinner's behaviorism suggests that man is more *reactive* than calculative and that he reacts to underlying properties of basic satisfactions and deprivations.

THE LATER YEARS. Beginning in 1958 with his first formal argument for a theory of social exchange,[39] and then in 1961 in the first edition of *Social Behavior: Its Elementary Forms,*[40] Homans' diverse influences mature into a coalescence that often hides the distinct elements that compose it.

In these works (the essential ones for the argument developed in this chapter), Homans attempts to augment his descriptive concepts (activity, sentiment, interaction, norm) with an operationalizing motif which allows for their development in *observable* and *testable* form. By introducing variable properties of the descriptive concepts, for example, along lines of *quantity, value* and *rate,* Homans hopes to provide a means of measurement. The key to this elaboration of theory is Homans' discovery of behaviorism.

In the end, a student of social behavior must be more interested in what men do than in what they say about what they do.[41]

We believe that the propositions of behavioral psychology are the general explanatory propositions of all the social sciences.[42]

For Homans, behaviorism provided the means for "explanation"—that is, the capability of reduction-to-cause for all human social behavior.[43] The essentials of Homans' argument are contained in several "propositions" that attempt to specify in behavioral terms why men do what they do.

The "success proposition":

For all actions taken by persons, the more often a particular action of a person is rewarded, the more likely the person is to perform that action.[44]

The "stimulus proposition":

If in the past the occurrence of a particular stimulus, or set of stimuli, has been the occasion on which a person's action has been rewarded, then the more similar the present stimuli are to the past ones, the more likely the person is to perform the action, or some similar action, now.[45]

The "value proposition":

The more valuable to a person is the result of his action, the more likely he is to perform the action.[46]

The "deprivation-satiation proposition":

The more often in the recent past a person has received a particular reward, the less valuable any further unit of that reward becomes for him.[47]

23

The "aggression-approval propositions":

> When a person's action does not receive the reward he expected, or receives punishment he did not expect, he will be angry; he becomes more likely to perform aggressive behavior, and the results of such behavior become more valuable to him.
>
> When a person's action receives reward he expected, especially a greater reward than he expected, or does not receive punishment he expected, he will be pleased; he becomes more likely to perform approving behavior, and the results of such behavior become more valuable to him.[48]

The "rationality proposition":

> In choosing between alternative actions, a person will choose that one for which, as perceived by him at the time, the value, V, of the result, multiplied by the probability, p, of getting the result, is the greater.[49]

With these propositions Homans claims to have articulated the "elementary" (in one sense, "fundamental") social processes. He wears the label of "reductionist," claiming that any level of institutional analysis is reducible to his elementary propositions.[50]

In the next section I will examine Homans' claim of reduction-to-cause to see how effective this program is in dealing with such basic issues as the nature of human interaction and the relationship between the individual and the institutional level in society.

Reductionism: A Search for Basic Properties

> We assume now . . . that though much emerges in social behavior, and is emerging all the time, which goes beyond any thing we can observe in the behavior of isolated individuals, yet nothing emerges that cannot be explained by propositions about the individuals as individuals, together with the given condition that they happen to be interacting. The characteristics of social groups and societies are

the resultants, no doubt the complicated resultants, but still the resultants, of the interaction between individuals over time—and they are no more than that.[51]

The substance of Homans' position is that societal forms and structures are nothing more than the composition effects of the sum of individuals pursuing self-interest—and, that the directions and formations resultant from this fact are "explainable" (cautiously halting with any suggestion of "predictable") by referring to psychological properties "basic" to man. In this section, I will maintain that little, if anything, having to do with the economics of reward and punishment, is "basic" to man; we propose that Homans' own work suggests this in the sense that he is unable, contrary to his claim, to "explain" elementary social exchange behavior without reference to institutionalized social facts. Next, I claim that Homans accepts as "givens" properties that must *emerge* from a dialectic between man and the nature of his existence and that the direction of emergence is not assured, but that it is a result of historical conditions. Finally, I will, in substance, claim that Homans, ironically, is not *enough* reductionist and falls into the same trap as those "institutional" sociologists with whom he differs.

To begin, we need to note a crucial element that remains consistent in Homans' exchange argument from the first edition to the revised edition of *Social Behavior*. In both editions, Homans goes to great pains to maintain the seeming purity of the behaviorist paradigm he adopts from Skinner (even to the extent of including in the 1961 edition a section on the conditioning of pigeons). In the context of this "radical" behaviorism, Homans appears to divest man of some essentially human properties—consciousness, calculation and voluntarism. Homans' model of man stipulates that man unwittingly reflects the impact of reward and punishment conditioning; his behavior, except for obvious physiological dissimilarities, is not so different from that of the pigeon. Animal behaviorism and human behaviorism bespeak the same process applied to different "organisms."

... given the differences in what is learned and in the capacity for learning, the behavior of the two organisms [man and pigeon] may still be similar in what happens after learning has taken place—similar especially in that both may illustrate just those propositions relating the frequency of activities and the state of the organism.[52]

Homans seems to have left man with little more than his ability to respond to stimuli. He has lost his conscious, deliberative capabilities.

If "rational" behavior means conscious rather than unconscious behavior, the question of rationality is irrelevant for us ... man's behavior can be utterly economic without his being any more conscious of what he is doing than the pigeon is.[53]

The argument with Homans is not that he has dehumanized man but, that in claiming to he has, in fact, indicated the impossibility of doing so.

Evidence for this claim is the error Homans makes in confusing the time properties of human action. Essentially, man is posited as a creature who, according to the tenets of behaviorism, acts in the present with "reference" *only* to the *past*. In other words, man and the pigeon are reflective of conditioning (learning) effects insofar as *past* learning is the primary, if not exclusive determinant of present behavior. The difficulty of maintaining a view such as this when dealing with higher order organisms is made apparent when such concepts as *cost* and *reward* are introduced into the model. For a pigeon the term reward is merely descriptive of primary needs-satisfaction properties—getting food or water, the cessation of pain, etc. For humans, however, introducing the concepts of cost and reward introduces man's unique capability to symbolize through *subjective processes*. Man's rewards are not limited to things from the past, he is capable of *expecting* and *anticipating* things of the *future* (perhaps even *new* situations with *new* rewards). Man *imputes, guesses, deliberates, makes choices*—all based on expectations, or symbolic representations of eventualities.[54] In his recent work Peter Ekeh[55] stipulates the properties of symbolic behavior and contrasts them with the properties of conditioned behavior.

1. In conditioned behavior, past experiences are necessary conditions of present activities . . . . On the other hand, in symbolic behavior, past experiences are neither necessary nor sufficient conditions of present activities.
2. Symbolic behavior is behaviorally creative; conditioned behavior is static.
3. Symbolic behavior is normative behavior shared by persons within a value system; conditioned behavior is non-normative behavior and is an attribute of the individual . . . .
4. Symbolic behavior makes use of time and space conceptions; on the other hand conditioned behavior cannot make use of time and space conceptions.[56]

This symbolic/subjective element also sneaks into Homans' concepts of "fair exchange"[57] and "distributive justice."[58] Both these concepts refer to *perceptions* of equality of return vis-à-vis investments. In order to perceive "equality," Homans' man *must* tacitly be allowed the capability of individual evaluation and consideration—not just the effects of conditioning.[59]

> If individual has any meaning in social exchange it is in the fact that the individual arrives at conclusions on the basis of . . . interpersonal comparisons.[60]

In addition to the symbolic/subjectivist element of choice processes there is also an institutionalized quality to Homans' conceptualization of distributive justice. It is inconceivable that reward maximization in a Hobbesian sense would not prevail if it were not for some element of normative propriety basic to perceptions of "fair exchange." Gouldner, for example, has identified a "norm of reciprocity" that he feels is endemic to social exchange.[61] A cognitive psychology, like that which Homans, in actuality, presents must recognize that some procedures and behaviors are maintained by more than mere conditioning—some element of *prescriptive action* must be present to provide realistic value bases from which to choose actions. While the behavioral aspect of Homans' exchange theory stipulates that man will, within realistic limits, pursue self-interest, it does *not* explain human social behavior. For an explanation to be complete, we must know, not only the dynamic of the process of choice but also the historical substance of choice—that is, *why* men pursue self-interest and how has this become (even in the virtual conditioned reflex version Homans employs) the dynamic that exchange theory claims is "basic" to human nature. I suggest the answers to these questions are not to be found in individual psychology but in a view of man that puts him in his context or milieu—his history. C. Wright Mills commented on just this issue at a time when behavioral sociology was in its infancy.

> The life of an individual cannot be adequately understood without references to the institutions within which his biography is enacted . . . the motivations of men, and even the varying extents to which various types of men are typically aware of them, *are to be understood in terms of the vocabularies of motive that prevail in a society and of social changes and confusions among such vocabularies. . . . When we understand social structures and structural changes as they bear upon more intimate scenes and experiences, we are able to understand the causes of individual conduct and feelings of which man in specific milieux are themselves unaware* . . . the human variety is such, that no 'elemental' psychologies, no theory of 'instincts' no principles of 'basic human nature' of which we know, enables us to account for the enormous human variety of types and individuals . . . to attempt to explain it in terms of a theory of 'basic human nature' is to confine human history itself in some arid little cage of concepts about 'human nature'—as often as not constructed from some precise and irrelevant trivialities about mice in a maze.[62]

While Homans steadfastly denies the existence of any normative element existent on bases other than individual self-interest,[63] his work seems to indicate the presence of a standard of fair exchange which is, at least in part, self-supportive through means certainly more generalized than the immediacy of other-sanctioned or other-rewarded behavior. To expect that reward commensurate with investments is "only fair" is to appeal to an *ethic*— not a situationally operationalized payoff matrix—but an ethic of fairness.

Two elements have been suggested in the preceding. First, that Homans' social exchange involves a symbolic, cognitive psychology and is not, as he claims, restricted to the "laws" of behaviorism. And, second, that as a cognitive psychology it presents the reality of a partly institutionalized format in the form of accepted standards by which exchange behavior will be adjudged as "fair."[64]

It perhaps would now be appropriate to attempt an explanation of where and how Homans "went wrong." How is it possible for him to illegitmately juxtapose man the organism, merely reactive to an input of stimuli, with man the deliberative, cognitive, predictive being who chooses among rewards and costs and who is capable of normatively evaluating fair exchange? The answer to this question may be found in the early history of Homans' sociological training under the influences of Pareto, Henderson and Murray. Two strains of thought represented by these three men seem directly responsible for Homans' peculiar model of man. One begins with Pareto's distinction between "logical" and "non-logical" behavior, later reflected with Henderson's work. The second is Murray's elaboration of human "needs." We previously accounted for these influences in Homans' early training at Harvard. What I now propose is to suggest that the unique combination of these influences enabled Homans, years later, to construct a theoretical portrait of human social behavior that includes a troublesome dual model of man in which he is seen simultaneously as a reactive organism and (at least, by unavoidable implication) a rational and calculating being.

In *Introduction to Pareto* (1934), Homans suggests that observers of society have consistently failed to account for the irrationalities in the world because "they have been unable to set up any broad theory of the non-logical action of men, the most important element determining the form of society."[65] Homans introduces

Pareto's sociology as a successful attempt in this direction. By adopting Pareto, Homans indicates an early representation of his career-long concern with the less than rational actions of men. At this stage, he is content to allow expression of this concern through such Paretian concepts as "residues," the manifestations of underlying sentiments, "derivations," or rationalizations for these sentiments, and "interests," or appetites, tastes and impulses. We stated earlier that Homans would eventually develop from these conceptualizations his properties, "sentiments" and "givens." What Homans has derived from Pareto then is what Henderson calls "a scientific description and logical analysis of the influence of the sentiments upon human affairs."[66] Henderson further notes:

> the actions of men are . . . in great part determined by the residues. Accordingly the exhibition of the residues, no less than eating, drinking, or breathing, may be recognized as a major function of the human organism. It is therefore necessary to take note that the role of the residues, or, speaking theoretically, of the sentiments that they manifest, is at least as important as the role of the logical activities of man. Indeed nearly everything that is accounted noblest and best, and also worst, in the actions of men depends upon (i.e., is a function of) residues.[67]

So, according to Pareto and Henderson, residues are represen-tations of sentiments—basic to human behavior. It should be emphasized that Pareto does not intend the terms, "residue" and "sentiment," to be interchangeable; they are not the same thing. Primary among their differences is the level of analysis obtainable by investigating each. Residues are recognizable as what Raymond Aron calls "certain consistencies" among acts or behavior.[68] As such they are open to study as real observable phenomena. And Pareto's formula for science was that it must restrict itself to that which is observable—to reality. Sentiments, on the other hand, are states of mind and as such are not directly observable. In effect, then, Pareto suggests that states of mind are not observable

30

but, they are approachable through a study of expressions of sentiments in a pre-behavioral mode—that is, through residues.

What does Homans make of all this? In *Introduction to Pareto*[69], he notes,

> We observe that men act in more or less similar ways and that these actions are more or less closely accompanied by certain statements more or less alike. We go on beyond our observations to assume that B, what men do, and C, what they say about what they do, are also in some undefined relationship with A, something for us very nebulus, their sentiments. But in order to make sociological theories we do not need to bother about A. All scientific theories need are facts, and of these we have a plenty, both B's and C's. A is merely a concession to common sense. Therefore the word "residues" will be used to mean "sentiments."[70]

What Homans wrote here (1934) is twofold. First, he indicated his own inability intellectually to pin down the concept of sentiment in human behavior—ironically, in spite of his career-long interest in non-logical behavior. And, he proposed to solve his dilemma by ignoring sentiments altogether (more specifically, lumping them into Pareto's residues, where they do not legitimately belong thus allowing sociology to get on with its task of observing the "observable facts" of social behavior. At this stage of his development, Homans was quite willing to share with us a "common-sense" understanding of sentiment.

In effect, what Homans has done with Pareto's tripartite depiction of human behavior as "expressions, acts, and states of mind" is to lop off the last, most difficult to approach aspect, and operationally to define it as if it were fully discernible as its own manifestation in action, that is, residues. This program would suffice for Homans for a number of years during which, with Henderson's advice, he was otherwise occupied immersing himself in the "historical method" so as to handle social science.

Our first clue that Homans might have been reconsidering his relegation of sentiment to pure behavior is found in what is ostensibly his least sociological work (the outgrowth of his study of history), *English Villagers of the Thirteenth Century*,[71] published seven years after his *Introduction to Pareto*. In this work Homans defines sentiment as "any psychological state,"[72] and credits this claim to the "conceptual scheme of V. Pareto."[73] So, Homans portrays Pareto's sentiments and residues (combined as they are in Homans' scheme) as psychological states. But is this rendition entirely creditable to Pareto's conceptual apparatus or has Homans added a new element to it? I suggest that Pareto would first of all not allow a combination of sentiment and residues; he would argue that one is a state of mind, the other a constant element in phenomena such as behaviors and expressions. Also, Pareto would insist, as Aron claims, "The study of the sentiments themselves is the province of the psychologist and not of the sociologist."[74] By claiming sentiments to be "psychological states," Homans has gone beyond his earlier dismissal of the concept as a matter of "common sense" and has hinted, at least, at the direction he might take in the future. Homans has at least payed lip service to sentiment as an important element of human behavior open to social science investigation. In fact, the concept plays (along with "interests"—another psychological concept) an important part in his *English Villagers*.[75]

It appears that Homans had discovered psychology, a psychology that allowed him to treat sentiment as a constituent and an *approachable* element in human social behavior. This last point is crucial, for if we recall Homans' Paretian orientation, sociology must deal with statements that are logico-experimental; that is, which are deducible from the observable. Homans' difficulty until now with sentiment had been that it is more "common-sense" than factually and observably real. The psychology that would enable Homans to conceptualize sentiments as real is the psychological need-structure of Henry A. Murray. Murray, we might recall, had a considerable influence on personality theory at Harvard during Homans' early years there. It would be inconceivable that Homans could have escaped his influence; indeed, we, will see much in Homans that bears direct reference to Murray's psychology.

As previously noted, Murray distinguished between two classes of needs: viscerogenic, having to do with physical satisfactions; and psychogenic, having to do with mental or emotional satisfactions. What is important here is Murray's claim that the psychogenic needs *derive from* the viscerogenic. In effect, Murray is proposing some kind of a biological basis for sentiment. We need only to look at some examples of Murray's psychogenic needs to see how far his proposal reaches from biology into areas usually depicted as sentiment. The following represent his lengthy list:[76] recognition, infavoidance (to avoid failure, shame), dominance, deference, aggression and abasement. For Homans, interested as he must have been at the time in methodologically approaching sentiment, a psychology that suggested a link between biological and psychological needs must have been appealing. It would be no great jump from the "states of mind" of Pareto's "sentiments" to the operationalizing motif of Murray's "psychogenic needs." Murray's contribution to an emerging social exchange theory is all the more notable when we recall that part of his orientation involved subscribing to the belief that persons tend to avoid pain and pursue pleasure. As Murray himself states, the obvious conclusion is that the "activity of drives tends to be hedonistically positive."[77]

Homans then had in his possession a Paretian interest in a sociology of "real" phenomena that recognized the presence of some underlying motive structure (sentiments), but which was not equipped to deal with it methodologically, and a psychology that related these sentiments to properties of real biological needs. Homans, the methodologist, and Homans, the student of human behavior, could now be joined. It was indeed possible to approach the *why* of human social behavior without lapsing into abstractions. In his autobiographical comments Homans notes his conception of psychological explanations. They are "in terms of the behavior of men *as* members of a species."[78] It is no coincidence that Homans, a man of considerable precision of terms, should describe psychology with words that undeniably create a tone of a species-biological-need structure. Through the use of this psychology (and a soon-to-be-discovered Skinnerian behaviorism) Homans was able to proceed with his conception of man as an organism responsive to a psychological-need structure that itself is rooted in basic and real biological properties.

As important as biological needs may be in grounding the derivation of psychological needs, they are not in themselves sufficient to deal with men in social situations. Homans' evolving theorizing recognized and adjusted for the necessity of elevating the "givens" of need structures from the physiological basics of food and drink to a utility on a more social level. Homans chooses, as an intermediary step on his way to men in a social world, the pigeon in a laboratory. As best enunciated in his 1961 edition of *Social Behavior,* Skinnerian behaviorism seems to Homans to be the key to understanding human behavior. For one thing, it provides Homans with a claim for reduction-to-cause (in its pure experimental form, Skinnerian behaviorism deals with little more than the very basic physiological needs of an organism); then, once Homans makes the claim that men and pigeons respond similarly to basic need satisfactions[79] it seems no great chore for Homans to replace pigeon needs with human needs and plug man into his behavioral model of operant conditioning.[79] This step, however, brings us to a major weakness of Homans' model.

Implicit in any behavioral model is a tacit acceptance of the fact that organisms have needs. If this were not so then no learning process that deals in rewards and punishments could be effective. When behaviorists in laboratories experiment with animals, they utilize the need-structure of the organism as a *given.* By manipulating the satisfaction, satiation or deprivation of the organism's needs, the experimenter seeks to manipulate its behavior. However, this process is possible only because the experimenter can count on the animals' capability of suffering deprivation of basic needs, (if he ever encountered a pigeon which didn't need to eat, or sleep, or drink, he could "teach" it little if anything). Obviously these needs *are so basic* to organisms that behaviorism in the manner of B. F. Skinner is possible.

Homans also assumes that some needs are "given," however he deals with men in social situations; therefore the type of need must be elevated from the physiological basics of food and drink to *utility on a more social level*. The problem begins here. As soon as Homans leaves the "psychologisms" of *physiological drive states* and enters the realm of the *social utility* of reward, he necessarily moves a big step upward from reduction-to-basic needs. There is nothing implicitly wrong with this change in level of analysis as long as one specifies what the new level of need structure is and where it comes from;[80] Homans omits this. However, in the 1974 edition of *Social Behavior,* Homans gives examples of the research findings which support his propositions. We see that he includes the following among satisfactions of human needs: "liking" (pp. 177–188); "approval" (pp. 119–122); "agreement" (p. 122); "consonance . . . with the group" (p. 124, pp. 127–130); "the maintenance of personal integrity" (p. 125). We immediately notice that satisfactions of this order are remote from the "basics" of an organism's physiology. These are essentially *social* rewards—that is, they are rewarding insofar as man exists among a community of men. While food and drink is always basic to an organism, Homans makes certain states seem basic although their rewarding nature may not at all be dependent on needs basic to the *organism* but may indeed be premised on *needs* derived from man's culture.[81] What Homans seems to be doing is integrating the lessons of behaviorism with a recollection of things from the past—specifically, Murray's derivation of psychogenic needs from viscerogenic needs. The problem with such a linkage is that the needs which Homans posits (e.g., liking, approval, etc.) as descriptive of man's make-up, may, indeed, not be nearly so basic as the primary needs of the pigeon. And, if they are not directly returnable to basic biology, then we must look elsewhere. What many sociologists would suggest is to seek their origin not in man himself, but in his society.

What I am suggesting is that before accepting a behaviorism

premised on a utility and reward structure, using needs for "liking" and "approval" as basic properties, it is essential to derive these properties and not assume them a priori. Like Schutz, I hold that:

> what we call the world of objective meaning is . . . abstracted in the social sphere from the constituting process of meaning-endowing consciousness, be this one's own or another's.[82]

The task then would appear to be to derive from historical conditions the "process of meaning-endowing" that has resulted in the human needs for approval and liking to have emerged and become capable of satisfaction through objects of the external world. In any attempt in this direction we would (with Marx[83]) specify a basic lesson of the dialectic—that is, that no concept itself (e.g., "need satisfactions") is a sufficient starting point for analysis; what is needed is a larger context, a "totality." I would think that "liking" and "approval," along with other need-satisfactions in Homans' theory, have attained "exchange-value"[84] in the sense that they are the currency of social relations often existing in states of scarcity in a market where their "surplus value" is unequally distributed.[85] They have attained an existence as need-objects, different from physiological needs in origin, but ultimately, perhaps just as crucial. According to Marx:

> Man is not only a natural being; he is a *human* natural being; i.e., he is a being for himself and hence a *species being*, as which he must confirm and realize himself both in his being and in his knowing. Consequently, *human* objects are not natural objects as they immediately present themselves . . .[86]

Marx's lesson in the dialectic is that man is both the product of and the producer of his objective environment—nothing (apart from his biology) is given; and, in the historical process of objectification, man's behavior creates a world. The world as created emerges with respect to historical, social, economic and political conditions. Man is never free of interests—represented as either deterministic economic conditions or class-dominated modes of thought.[87] These are the lessons Homans has not incorporated into his thinking; if he had he could not claim, when dealing with utilities and rewards as he does, to have reduced "sociological propositions" to the "propositions of learning theory in psychology" and thus, to have "brought men back in." In his effort to bring men back in, Homans has ignored the actual causes for the variations that occur in forms of social behavior. The capability of appreciation of rewards and punishments that are not endemic to the human organism must emerge socially. Having identified the rewards, Homans' next, and essential, task is to trace their development.

We have seen that the person whom Homans displays for us is not just a reactive organism whose reference is only the here and now as it is conditioned by the past; rather, man is depicted as a being who is capable of symbolizing eventualities in the future. Homans, therefore, is not restricting himself, as he claims, to elementary social behavior, but is, in fact, opening up the exchange network to include such aspects (e.g., a behaviorly creative orientation to the future, and, a normatively prescriptive value base) as would allow for a model of man in an institutionalized setting. Homans' dilemma is that while his sociology and his model of man refuse to allow him to remain at the "elementary" level, he insists on minimizing, if not totally denying, any institutional, "social fact" level of analysis. He relies for his "explanation" of human social behavior on a model that requires certain properties (e.g., psychological needs) be assumed as "given" so that a bridge may be constructed between the "what" of man's acts and the "why" of his motivations.

Homans' failure to deal exclusively with elementary behavior and, thus, his failure at explanation is evident in his unsuccessful attempt at restricting elementary social behavior to a dyad. If this were possible, then Homans' sole emphasis on reward/punishment causation would make sense. If Homans could limit social exchange to an ego-alter confrontation he would obtain the immediacy necessary to demonstrate that people do often respond to the short-term returns on their behaviors. However, if Homans opens up exchange in the sense of Lévi-Strauss' "generalized exchange," he will be admitting to the game such *symbolic* elements as "foregone rewards" (cost), social approval, money and justice. Once the exchange involves itself with symbolic elements it necessarily utilizes institutionalized parameters of reward and value. Let us then see how successful Homans is in limiting exchange to a dyad. Apparently he is not quite successful at all. In spite of renaming it "multiple dyadic exchanges,"[88] or "indirect exchange,"[89] Homans does not conceal the fact that he is dealing in almost all of his examples with *networks* of multi-person, *generalized* exchange behavior.

The effect of expanding dyadic relationships to triads has been explored by Georg Simmel.[90] Simmel recognizes that one result of expansion to triads is the generalization of what previously was a single face-to-face responsibility. The effect produced is the capability of objectification into "real" things, among them, a general moral code. Berger and Luckmann have also commented on this property of triads.[91]

> As long as the nascent institutions are constructed and maintained only in the interaction of A and B, their objectivity remains tenuous, easily changeable, almost playful, even while they attain a measure of objectivity by the mere fact of their formation . . . A and B alone are responsible for having constructed this world. A and B remain capable of changing it or abolishing it. . . . All this changes in the process of transmission to the new generation (triad). The objectivity of the institutional world "thickens" and "hardens" not only for the children, but . . . for the parents as well. . . . A world so regarded attains a firmness in consciousness; it becomes real in an even more massive way.[92]

An additional reference for the effects of expansion to triads is the social-psychology of George Herbert Mead.[93] For Mead, the beginning of an objectified institutionalized essence to the world of the self was in its extension of the "significant other" as a reference for propriety to a "generalized other"—a triadic representation that includes a general moral code.

We see, then, that Homans' inability to restrict social exchange to dyads has in effect paved the way for extending social exchange theory from elementary behavior to a level where "social facts" obtain a "thing-like" nature—that is, to the level of objectification,[94] a level to which Homans will not climb.

CONCLUSION AND EVALUATION

In this section I propose to restate the general argument developed in the preceding discussion. However, in an attempt to provide a more lucid continuity of the essentials I offer a narrative that is relatively unencumbered by the distractions of quotations and footnotes. All of what we will suggest here, however, is provided for by documentation, presented earlier.

In addition, I will reintroduce an argument that is not yet fully developed. The reasons for this are twofold: the argument articulates a major consequence of the deficiencies of Homans' exchange theory and also should provide a transition to the concerns of the next chapter.

Homans' Intellectual Continuity

In the introduction to this chapter I proposed to show that Homans' sociology displays an intellectual continuity of a particular line of thought. While that line of thought has crystallized at several points along its development into such forms as a social psychology of needs and a theory of social exchange, these are, like buds along a vine, only representations of what is running through the stem. Homans' career has been the continuous development of two major issues. The first is a methodological concern for the establishment of a sociology that will serve to reduce explanation of human social behavior to a level sufficiently elementary so that basic and universal properties will be identifiable. The second, necessarily related, issue is Homans' career-long attempt at identifying the non-logical, emotional and psychological elements in human behavior. In effect, these two goals are parallel and at times, identical in nature. For, if Homans is successful in identifying the elements he claims underlie all human behavior, he also will have produced a model based on reduction-to-cause. Let us now retrace the directions Homans has taken with the development of these two concerns and decide how successful he has been with each.

At the outset of his training, Homans found in the sociology of Pareto a substantiation of what he was already prepared to believe. What, in fact, he found was an elaboration of a model of non-logical behavior in which "sentiments," "appetites," "impulses" and "states of mind" were clearly depicted as being at the root of human behavior. Needless to say, Pareto provided reinforcement for Homans' views (especially since Pareto's attempt was at doing *real* science based on *real* observations of *real* phenomena). The primary difficulty for Homans in adopting Pareto's sociology was, in fact, Pareto's inability or disinterest in actually dealing with sentiment as a phenomenon for investigation. He was content to articulate its place in the scheme of human action but did little more than describe its apparent existence before concentrating on its manifestations in residues. Perhaps Pareto's accomplishment in classifying the manifestations of sentiment would have sufficed for another fledgling sociologist, but Homans was apparently not content with leaving the concept to a matter of "common sense." What Homans sought was a real basis upon which to ground his conception of sentiment, thus providing the empirical apparatus that would allow him to construct a deductive, law-like theory of all of human behavior.

We earlier suggested that Homans was quite likely influenced by the work of the humanistic psychologist, Henry A. Murray. Certainly Murray's work provided what Homans seemed to have lacked at this stage—that is, an empirical grounding of psychological needs (or, sentiments) along with a claim that human behavior is explainable by seeing it as the result of man's attempts at satisfying these basic needs. The influence of this perspective is woven through virtually all of Homans' later work, from "Bringing Men Back In," an essay in which he argues for a recognition in sociology of the humanness of the social actor who comes to us complete with interests and goals, to his later work in *Social Behavior* in which a behaviorist form is given to these needs or sentiments. Here they are presented to us in propositions that proclaim them as the imperatives behind an explanation of why men do what they do. In Murray, Homans would find additional support for his earlier conceptualization of man driven by the desire to satisfy a class of non-logical needs that provide the bases for human behavior.

Homans' explorations into cultural anthropology also served the development of his primary interests. In his critique (along with Schneider) of Lévi-Strauss' work, Homans reinforces the major thread in his emerging sociological theory—that people seek that which is rewarding. Homans takes Lévi-Strauss to task for suggesting that explanation of primitive marriage-patterning is obtainable by examining the effects on the social system. Homans suggests that not only is it bad form to argue backward from effects, but that since it is illegitimately teleological to do so, no explanation is possible. True science must explain from *causes* not effects, for only in this fashion can valid explanation be realized. Homans' alternative explanation is, for him perfectly logical; people seek satisfaction of affective needs (sentiment), and certain forms of marriage-patterning are more encouraging of this satisfaction than others. Here again, Homans has suggested the direction for his evolving search for universal laws of human behavior.

The last major stage in Homans' developing theory of social behavior is his adoption of Skinnerian behaviorism. Having attempted a rendition in *The Human Group* of empirically derived generalizations that would serve to describe human behavior, Homans now sees that mere description would not suffice. Although he was pleased with the level of description reached in this work, he felt the need to go beyond it and to establish a causal chain of deductively derived propositions that would provide both the reduction-to-cause and the universality necessary to claim them as a true theory of human behavior. In discovering the psychology of operant conditioning in Skinner's work Homans claims to have found the answer. Skinner provided Homans with an observable and testable motif by making possible variable properties of the descriptive concepts developed in *The Human Group*. From Skinner, Homans adopts the program of a learning theory which suggests a way of getting at the *why* of human behavior in a demonstrable and methodologically defensible fashion. The culmination of this merger of behaviorism with Homans' earlier formulated conceptions of a model of man as motivated by a drive for need satisfaction is the full-blown social exchange theory of *Social Behavior: Its Elementary Forms*. In this work Homans has reached what is for him a satisfactory level of explanation. He produced a theory whose development is along deductively causal lines and one that proports to have unearthed those principles that are elementary and universal in human behavior.

In the next sections, we will examine the primary achievements and defects of Homans' social exchange theory. As was noted in the introduction to this chapter, while we believe an exchange model of human behavior to be generally acceptable, Homans' variant is fraught with difficulties that both weaken its deductive underpinnings and limit the extent to which it is applicable as a general theory of society.

Achievements

In producing his social exchange theory Homans has made notable achievements in areas of the methodological development of a valuable theoretical strategy, the usefulness of the theory itself, and also in terms of a more heuristic benefit for sociology in general.

It is no accident that Homans' exchange model emerged in the late 1950s and early 1960s. This followed a period of American sociology when the grand theory of Parsonian functionalism dominated in many sociological circles.[95] The deficiencies inherent in this model inspired critics to offer their rendition of what the social world was really like. George Homans was one of the most prolific of these critics. His primary objection to functionalism was the teleological nature of its attempt at explanation. Functionalists, Homans argued, were not "explaining" at all; they could not, for they depended on an after-the-fact analysis of effects and did not adequately produce an understanding of the *causes* of social phenomena. In his way, Homans is, responsible in great measure, for whatever limitations on explanation from consequence have come about since the 1950s. Along with a number of other sociologists (many of whom went off in directions quite different from Homans', e.g., conflict theory, neo-Marxism), Homans has, by specifying what theory should be, given sociology a more legitimate explanatory base. In managing this, Homans has contributed to the advantages derived from reducing the level of theoretical abstraction from the "grand" theory of Parsons to a more empirically-grounded level.

Notable as these achievements may be, they are, after all, more heuristic than specific, and furthermore, do not exhaust the extent of Homans' contribution. He *has produced* a deductive system with some measure of empirical grounding that has a specific, though perhaps limited, *use* to *explain* human social behavior. Whatever its faults, and there are some, Homans has, I believe, accurately depicted human social behavior as explainable by the tenets of social exchange. Let us now explore them.

Homans' version of sociological theory has focused attention on a number of important exchange issues. First, Homans has produced a model of man that I would suggest is both realistic and empirically defensible; man is to be seen as an agent with his own interests and goals—with an orientation toward the achievement and satisfaction of these interests and goals. He typically enters into relationships of negotiation with other men who have their own interests and goals and who similarly are motivated by the attempt to satisfy them. In the process of pursuing his own interests man, must, as Mead noted, "take the other into account." In terms of exchange processes this involves give and take, which may, in some instances be either all of one or all of the other. The possible outcomes from this exchange are multi-varied. Depending on situation, resources, abilities, competences and so forth, different measures of success or failure in the pursuit of one's own interests will result.

Homans has contributed to an emphasis in contemporary sociology on the subjectivity of the actor. We earlier claimed that Homans' psychology of man is a cognitive one in spite of the behavioral orientation of the Skinnerian model he adopts. As such it depicts the subjective, evaluative processes of the actor as he reckons with the variations in his environment that affect his life chances. Homans' actor is an economic man who attempts to control the marketplace, his competitors and his own maneuvering for advantage. While he may occasionally be powerless to influence the elements in that economy, he is, for the most part, aware of the costs and profits available there and what actions he must attempt so as to strike a successful balance.

Finally, Homans has made a notable contribution to the identification, description and categorization of the needs and rewards determinative of man's social behavior. By noting such elements as "liking," "approval," "agreement," "consonance with the group" and "the maintenance of personal integrity," and by describing the nature of their effects on human behavior, Homans has provided a useful explanatory scheme. A combination of these "causes," along with an awareness of the dynamics of the exchange process directed toward their achievement or satisfaction, constitutes a major contribution to an understanding of human behavior.

Defects

As is often the case, those elements that are the strengths of an argument are indicative of, if not contributory to, its weaknesses. In many ways with Homans' exchange theory we need only note its accomplishments to point out its defects. In general, the problems with Homans' sociology are due to his efforts at reducing analysis to a level where explanation of a causal nature is possible. The consequences of developing a tight argument on the "elementary" level have prevented Homans from a meaningful extension of his theory to an explanation of any social unit much larger than the two-member-direct exchange. Specifically, Homans' theory is weakest when it attempts explanation (to the extent that it even tackles the task) of such objectified and institutionalized social phenomena as power, authority, domination, exploitation and the general structural effects of organization, stratification and inequality.

Homans' cognitive model, in presenting man as a being driven by the imperative of need-satisfaction, stresses the subjective bases upon which the actor evaluates his and others' behavior as contributory to those satisfactions. "Value" then is the worth put on these actions by the actor himself. However, others have pointed out that value, perhaps more often than not, is not simply the property of the actor's evaluative capacity. Secord and Backman,[96] for example, record five sources for the changes in value that rewards and costs may undergo. All of them involve more than merely the actor's own immediacy of evaluation. These changes might occur:

1. relative to a history of exchanges (both the actor's own, and those of others of whom he is aware);
2. as members of a dyadic relationship change (a previous partner may take second place to a new, more valuable partner);
3. as the situation of the actor changes (age changes, for example);
4. within the same situation (as priorities may shift over time);
5. as actors give new meanings to old behaviors (thus, effectively, reevaluating them).

Secord and Backman, then, suggest that evaluation of rewards and costs is too complex a process only to see it as the domain of one actor's subjectivity.

Thibaut and Kelley[97] also point to the complexity of the evaluative process. They introduce the concept, "comparison levels," (standards by which to evaluate) and suggest that there are four types of human relationships—each based on a different complex of evaluative mechanisms. These are as follows:

1. A relationship where the actor's pay off (reward) is *higher* than a general comparison level (as determined by past experience of self and others), and *higher* than the comparison level for *alternative* relationships. This relationship, they suggest, is both stable and satisfying.
2. A relationship where the pay off is *higher* than the general comparison level, but *lower* than the comparison level for alternatives. This form of relationship is satisfying but not stable.
3. A relationship where the pay off is *lower* than the general comparison level, but *higher* than the comparison level for alternatives. Here the relationship is satisfying, but not stable.
4. A relationship where the pay off is *lower* than the general comparison level, and *lower* than the comparison level for alternatives. This relationship is neither stable, nor satisfying, and will probably dissolve.

What Thibaut and Kelley suggest is, again, that the bases of evaluation of rewards and costs are more complex than merely one actor exercising his subjectivity. In his attempt at providing a deductive model of human social behavior, Homans has ironed out the rough edges and left us with a being free to choose among evaluated alternatives (when, indeed, he has any), without the encumbrances of the complexities of the process of evaluation of these alternatives.

A major defect then in Homans' theory is the neglect of the effect of personal and institutional power on exchange choices. Homans' actor need only weigh the relative costs and rewards of options open to him and plot his course through waters that are seldom more turbulent than the ripples of individual skills and competencies at work. Homans minimizes and often overlooks

institutional manisfestations of power, authority and coercion—
often more accurately explanatory of actual behavior. Is it the
"choice" to obey that sends a man to the gallows or is he powerless
in the face of the state, the law and the gun? Homans, at times,
seems to deny the very existence of power. He suggests, for
example, that the law of "fair exchange" (distributive justice)
serves to neutralize profit maximization among those seeking
rewards. In *Social Behavior* (1974) he notes:

> ... There is a tendency in repeated exchanges between men for
> their power to equalize, so that neither will change his behavior
> toward the other any further. ... It is this process, more than any
> tendency to follow habit or custom, that maintains such stability as
> there is in the relations between men. That is, the condition of equal
> power is a condition of social equilibrium. ... The great bulk of
> controls over social behavior are not external but built into the
> relationships themselves. ...[98]

Homans' problem is that in his attempt to depict the dynamics
of direct exchange, he has closed off his pair of interactants from
the real world—a world, that is, in which people are not equal in
their "investments" or in their ability to "exchange," rather they
are differentiated and stratified at the outset. How can any fair
and just exchange take place while men exist with these inequities? When Homans attempts to deal with power, he does it in a
unique way. He does not allow for the *derivation* of power from
within the exchange network, rather he depicts it as a priori,
already held by some and *merely* utilized in interaction. Homans
notes that, "power, then, depends on the ability to provide rewards that are valuable because they are scarce."[99] Power here is
not depicted as an attribute that emerges from interaction but is
seen as a resource, presumably already well-established and
merely to be *used* in exchange.

In the end Homans produces a model of human behavior
useful for explaining (with certain limitations) the simplest forms
of direct exchange (that is, between only two actors). The model
fails, however, in any attempt at explaining anything approaching

society-wide structures. The central reason for this failure is that Homans does not provide for the *emergence* of more complex elements (e.g., authority, institutions and norms) from the exchange itself. While it may be useful to be able to "explain" why one actor will behave in a certain way with respect to one other actor, it would be far more useful to explain such complex phenomena as the evolution of relatively stable societal forms from the elementary properties of interaction. It is in the next chapter, which deals with the social exchange theory of Peter M. Blau, where such an attempt at extension to the institutional level will be examined.

NOTES

1. George C. Homans, "Social Behavior as Exchange," *American Journal of Sociology,* 63 (1958), pp. 597–606.
2. M. J. Mulkay, *Functionalism, Exchange and Theoretical Strategy* (New York: Schoken Books, 1971).
3. Peter P. Ekeh, *Social Exchange Theory; The Two Traditions* (Cambridge, Mass.: Harvard University Press, 1974).
4. Claude Lévi-Strauss, *Les Structures Elementaires de la Parente* (Paris: Presses Universitaires de France, 1949).
5. George C. Homans, "Bringing Men Back In," *American Sociological Review* 29 (1964), pp. 809–818.
6. George C. Homans, *Sentiments and Activities* (New York: The Free Press, 1962), p. 29.
7. George C. Homans, *Social Behavior: Its Elementary Forms* (New York: Harcourt, Brace & World, 1961), pp. 8–16.
8. George C. Homans, *The Human Group* (New York: Harcourt, Brace & World, 1950).
9. Vilfredo Pareto, *The Mind and Society* (New York: Dover Publications, Inc., 1963). Lawrence J. Henderson, *Pareto's General Sociology: A Physiologist's Interpretation* (New York: Russell & Russell, 1935). Henry A. Murray, *Explorations in Personality* (New York: Oxford Press, 1938).
10. Homans, *Sentiments and Activities,* p. 4.
11. Ibid., p. 8.
12. Pareto, *The Mind and Society,* p. 72.
13. Homans, "Bringing Men Back In," 1964.
14. Ibid., p. 818.
15. Ibid., p. 811. What Homans is specifying as sociological theory, Zetterberg has dealt with as "axiomatic theory" [see Hans L. Zetterberg, "On Axiomatic Theories in Sociology," in Zetterberg, *On Theory and Verifi-*

cation in Sociology (Stockholm: Almquist and Wiksell, 1954); also, Zetterberg, *On Theory and Verification in Sociology*, Revised edition (Totowa, New Jersey: The Bedminster Press, 1963)]. Axiomatic Theory specifies the nature of the relationships among variables in a logico-deductive model. So, for example, we can speak of the manner of deducing probabilities from related propositions:

> Proposition 1: The greater the A, the greater the B;
> Proposition 2: The greater the B, the greater the C;

from this we can logically deduce the probability, the greater the A, the greater the C.

As "correct form," axiomatic theory characterizes much of modern sociology. Proponents of this form can point to its apparent advantages in dealing with social phenomena, and critics seem equally adept in noting their exceptions to the deductive arguments. For example, a most convincing argument challenging the use of axiomatic theory in sociology comes from Costner and Leik ["Deductions from Axiomatic Theory," *American Sociological Review* 29 (December 1964), pp. 819–835]. The authors argue that the empirical reality of deductive causation is frequently not obtained in sociological theory. They maintain that deduction *cannot* be obtained without "high relationships" between propositions; in other words, claiming relationships between propositions (e.g., "positive" or "negative correlations") is not sufficient to ignite the deductive/causal chain. What is required are demonstrably *high* levels of correlation.

16. See Homans' autobiographical comments in *Sentiments and Activities*.
17. George C. Homans, and Charles P. Curtis, *An Introduction to Pareto: His Sociology* (New York: Howard Fertig, 1934, 1970).
18. Ibid., p. 5.
19. Ibid., p. 7.
20. Murray came to Harvard in 1927 as assistant to the psychopathologist, Morton Prince, where he was part of a clinic staff devoted to the study of personality. He was at Harvard, on and off, until his retirement in 1962.
21. Calvin S. Hall and Gardner Lindzey, *Theories of Personality* (New York: John Wiley and Sons, Inc., 1957), p. 161.
22. Salvatore R. Maddi and Paul T. Costa, *Humanism in Personology: Alport, Maslow and Murray* (Chicago: Aldine Atherton, Inc., 1972), p. 156.
23. Ibid., p. 85.
24. Pareto, *The Mind and Society*, p. 1406.
25. Murray, *Explorations in Personality*, pp. 123–124.
26. Ibid., pp. 76–77.
27. Ibid., p. 80.
28. Ibid.
29. Ibid., pp. 81–2.
30. Homans, *An Introduction to Pareto*, p. 225.
31. Herbert Spencer, *Social Statics* (London: Chapman, 1851).
32. Homans, *Sentiments and Activities*, p. 29.
33. See, for example, Spencer, *Social Statics*.
34. Homans, *Sentiments and Activities*, p. 247.

35. George C. Homans and David M. Schneider, *Marriage, Authority, and Final Causes: A Study of Unilateral Cross-Cousin Marriage* (New York: The Free Press, 1955) p. 15.

36. Homans, *The Human Group*, p. 133.

37. B. F. Skinner, *The Behavior of Organisms* (New York: Appleton-Century Crofts, 1938); *Science and Human Behavior* (New York: Macmillan, 1953).

38. Homans, *The Human Group*, p. 296 (my emphasis).

39. Homans, "Social Behavior as Exchange."

40. The "revised edition" of *Social Behavior* (1974) is, indeed, revised. Primarily, Homans has "tightened up" the argument by detailing aspects that critics of the 1961 edition found fault with. Major among these adjustments are the discussions of power and status. However as Homans himself says in the Preface to the revised edition, "it is not that I have much altered the substance of the underlying argument; rather, I have tried, in the light of criticism and my own further thinking, to tighten up the argument and to make it more lucid and logical."

41. Homans, *Social Behavior* (1974), p. 226.

42. Ibid., p. 67.

43. A striking paradox is the fact that Homans would choose Skinner's version of behaviorism. It is, among all the variants of the form, perhaps the *least* amenable to what Homans proposes to do, i.e., explain human social behavior. Skinner's version of behaviorism [Arthur Staats, "Skinnerian Behaviorism: Social Behaviorism or Radical Behaviorism?", *The American Sociologist* 11 (February, 1976), pp. 59–60, calls it a "radical behaviorism"] does not allow for essential human properties such as creativity, self-determination, freedom, feelings and cognitions (many of which are endemic to the Weberian subjectivist tradition). Staats maintains that other "social behaviorisms" would allow for these.

  Part of the paradox is the fact that Homans is occasionally accused of *violating* the Skinnerian model [Morton Deutsch, "Homans in the Skinner Box," *Sociological Inquiry* 34 (1969), pp. 156–165]. We maintain that the need to violate "radical" behaviorist propositions *indicates the need for a more flexible variant.*

44. Homans, *Social Behavior* (1974), p. 16.

45. Ibid., p. 22.

46. Ibid., p. 25.

47. Ibid., p. 29.

48. Ibid., p. 37.

49. Ibid., p. 43.

50. Ibid., p. 367.

51. Ibid., p. 12.

52. Homans, *Social Behavior*, 1961, p. 29.

53. Ibid., p. 80; also *Social Behavior*, 1974, pp. 48–49. It should be noted that another sociologist, M. Weber, might argue that "economic" behavior is impossible without action that is *zweckrational*, and that this necessarily implies consciousness.

54. Homans *has* admitted that behavioral psychology does include "the so-called theory of rational behavior" (i.e., choice), see, Homans, "The Sociological Relevance of Behaviorism," in Burgess and Bushwell, *Be-*

havioral Sociology, (New York: 1969), p. 13. However as late as 1974 in the revised edition of *Social Behavior* he seems to have ignored this momentary lapse from radical behaviorism, and reverted to his earlier position. We might also note that Parsons [see, Talcott Parsons, "Levels of Organization and the Mediation of Social Interaction," *Sociological Inquiry* 34 (1964), pp. 207–220.] maintains that economic exchanges are never "elementary," they always involve symbolized representations of property and contract.

55. Peter P. Ekeh, *Social Exchange Theory: The Two Traditions.*
56. Ibid., pp. 107–109.
57. Homans, *Social Behavior*, 1961, p. 72.
58. Homans, *Social Behavior*, 1974, pp. 241–268; *Social Behavior*, 1961, pp. 233–247.
59. Ekeh, (*Social Exchange Theory*, p. 130) suggests that the 1961 edition of *Social Behavior* is really two different books. "The first book ends at page 61 and deals with *profitable exchange*. The second book beings at page 72, and deals with *fair exchange*."
60. Ekeh, ibid., p. 130.
61. Alvin W. Gouldner, "The Norm of Reciprocity: A Preliminary Statement," *American Sociological Review* 25 (1960), pp. 161–179. It should be noted that Homans rejects the existence of such a norm in social exchange apart from a reward–punishment schedule to support it. (See Homans, *Social Behavior*, 1974, pp. 217–18).
62. C. Wright Mills, *The Sociological Imagination* (New York: Oxford University Press, 1959), pp. 161–164, (emphasis mine).
63. See Homans, *Social Behavior*, 1974, p. 218, e.g., "No norm enforces itself."
64. We note that there are non-cognitive, non-voluntaristic variants of exchange behaviorism. For example, see the work of Richard M. Emmerson, "Operant Psychology and Exchange Theory," pp. 379–405 in Robert L. Burgess and Don Bushwell, Jr. *Behavioral Sociology* (New York: Columbia University Press, 1969). Also, "Exchange Theory, Part II; Exchange Relations, Exchange Networks and Groups as Exchange Systems" in Joseph Berger, Morris Zelditch, and Bo Anderson, eds., *Sociological Theories in Progress Vol. II*, (Boston: Houghton-Mifflin, 1972).
65. Homans and Curtis, *An Introduction to Pareto*, p. 7.
66. Henderson, *Pareto's General Sociology*, p. 7.
67. Ibid., pp. 24–25.
68. Raymond Aron, *Main Currents in Sociological Thought*, (New York: Basic Books, Inc., 1967) Vol II, p. 118.
69. Homans, *An Introduction to Pareto*, p. 81.
70. Ibid., p. 88.
71. George C. Homans, *English Villagers of the Thirteenth Century*, (New York: Russell and Russell, 1941).
72. Ibid., p. 376.
73. Ibid., p. 457, n. 48.
74. Aron, *Main Currents*, p. 122.
75. See especially Chapter XVIII.
76. Murray, *Explorations in Personality*, pp. 81–82.

77. Ibid., p. 90.
78. Homans, *Sentiments and Activities*, p. 33, (emphasis mine).
79. See, for example, Homans, *Social Behavior*, 1961, p. 29.
80. See Bengt Abrahamsson, "Homans on Exchange: Hedonism Revisited," *American Journal of Sociology* 76 (1970), pp. 273–285, for a critique which notes the vagueness of Homans' "utilities" and "rewards."
81. Dennis Wrong's classic "The Oversocialized Conception of Man in Modern Sociology" *American Sociological Review*, 26 (1961) deals with the illegitimate assumption that man is essentially an "approval-seeker" and subsumes all other motives to this one.
82. Alfred Schutz, *The Phenomenology of the Social World*, trans. G. Walsh and F. Lehnert (Evanston, Ill.: Northwestern University Press, 1967), pp. 4–6.
83. See Karl Marx, *A Contribution to the Critique of Political Economy* (London: Lawrence and Wishart, 1971).
84. Karl Marx, *Theories of Surplus Value*, VOL. III (London: Lawrence and Wishart: 1972) pp. 268–269.
85. Ibid.
86. Karl Marx, "Economic and Philosophical Manuscripts." *Early Writings* (New York: Vintage Books, 1975), p. 391.
87. See Karl Mannheim, *Ideology and Utopia* (New York: Harcourt Brace Jovanovich, 1936).
88. Homans, *Social Behavior*, 1961, pp. 84–85.
89. Ibid., p. 385.
90. Georg Simmel, *The Sociology of Georg Simmel*, pp. 138–142; 145–169.
91. Peter L. Berger and Thomas Luckmann, *The Social Construction of Reality: A Treatise in the Sociology of Knowledge* (Garden City, New York: Doubleday Anchor Books, 1967).
92. Ibid., p. 58.
93. See George Herbert Mead, *Mind, Self and Society* (Chicago: University of Chicago Press, 1962).
94. Ironic is the discovery that Homans' early work (e.g., *The Human Group*) often disclosed elements of a true collectivist tradition not unlike those of Comte and Durkheim. For example: "If we examine the motives we usually call individual self-interest, we shall find that they are, for the most part, neither individual nor selfish but that they are, the product of group life and serve the ends of a whole group not just an individual . . . that both self-interest *and* something else are satisfied by group life is the truth . . . as Mayo says, "If a number of individuals work together to achieve a common purpose, a harmony of interests will develop among them to which individual self-interest will be sub-ordinated. This is a very different doctrine from the claim that individual self-interest is the solitary human motive." (*The Human Group*, pp. 95–96).
95. Benton Johnson, *Functionalism in Modern Sociology: Understanding Talcott Parsons* (Morristown, New Jersey: General Learning Press, 1975) p. 1, claims, "Until the early 1950s it was widely suspected that Parsons and his students were charting the future course for all sociology."
96. P. F. Secord and C. W. Backman, *Social Psychology* (New York: McGraw-Hill, 1964), p. 262.

97. J. W. Thibaut and H. H. Kelley, *The Social Psychology of Groups* (New York: Wiley, 1959), Chapters 2 and 6.
98. Homans, *Social Behavior,* 1974, p. 76.
99. George C. Homans, "Fundamental Social Processes," in Neil J. Smelser, ed., *Sociology* (New York: Wiley and Sons, 1967), p. 55.

T H R E E : : *An Extension of Social Exchange Theory : Peter M. Blau*

INTRODUCTION

With the publication in 1961 of Homans' *Social Behavior: Its Elementary Forms,* social exchange took its place in contemporary sociological theory. Subsequent years saw numerous efforts to implement Homans' model as an explanatory guide to researching the world of human interaction. In addition, some attempts have been made to elaborate, embellish or modify the exchange tenets articulated in Homans' work. Some (e.g., Emerson)[1] attempted to fix social exchange more firmly in the propositions of operant conditioning, while other efforts sought to open up the model to include a broader picture of what constitutes social phenomena. Peter M. Blau is among the latter in these efforts.[2]

As with Homans (before him), Blau's social exchange theory shows the influence of several sources, primary among them is the work of Homans himself. Blau's work derives much of its uniqueness and originality from the very fact that the author was operating in a universe no longer theoretically or methodologically naive to the social exchange model. While Homans claimed more originality than he manifests and operated as if he were charting totally new courses,[3] Blau had to contend with the already entrenched existence of Homans' exchange theory. It is safe to say that Blau's work is, in a very real sense, an answer to questions left unanswered by Homans' theory. Much, then, of an understanding of Blau's work will involve a comparison with Homans'.

What Blau will elaborate on as the major failings of Homans' sociology are in no small measure due to the restrictiveness of the theoretical strategy that Homans adopts. Homans insists that his theory will be complete only when it forms a deductive system. While this is certainly an admirable methodological stance, it does require that Homans accept as given and unproblematic those social phenomena that lie outside his causal chain yet, nonetheless, do exist in the world of man. Such phenomena include norms, values, organizations, institutions and any other social structures whose complexities evade deciphering by the reductionism of operant conditioning.

Blau sets out with the intent "to derive complex from simpler processes without the reductionist fallacy of ignoring emergent properties."[4] While Blau sees the importance of reducing explanation to properties basic enough so as to discover law-like propositions of a universal quality, he also recognizes the impossibility of ever causally deriving complex structures by means only of such reductionism. What Blau envisions is a compromise, a mediation between individualistic sociologies, noting those of Goffman and Simmel[5] whose emphasis is on the everyday face-to-face interaction[6] of direct exchange[7] with more collectivist sociologies (Weber and Parsons are mentioned)[8] which begin with a study of the more complex structures.

In his efforts at mediation Blau makes a meaningful substitution. He throws out the operant conditioning of Homans and replaces it with an equally reductionist formulation of economics. By doing this, Blau suggests a way of getting at the emergence of complex structures. I will suggest in the argument that follows that while Blau succeeds in erasing the unproblematic "givens" of Homans' exchange theory, he has written in his own non-problematics—that is, the operations of a social order whose rationality is assumed and *not* derived. He has thus, like Homans, painted a limited picture of the world; one which is only partially correct.

SOURCES AND ELABORATIONS

Basics: Blau and Homans

Peter Blau and George Homans are the two foremost representatives of contemporary social exchange theory. However, their statements suggest that they represent a considerable divergence on such issues as research strategy, scope of application and identification of essentials. Sometimes these claimed differences are actual; that is, they reflect real differences, often, however, what is claimed is not the same as what is done and the two authors effectively achieve similar ends.

Homans purports to do theory. While he does claim that his work is unfinished and does not fully deal with all societal phenomena,[9] he also maintains that "we need no new propositions to explain the new phenomena."[10] In other words, Homans is suggesting at least a *theoretical* completeness in his model. He claims to have produced all those propositions that are necessary to explain social behavior. In the last chapter I suggested that Homans' model is far from even theoretically complete and lacks, for one example, a deductive extension into the area of social structure, which would be necessary to achieve that completeness.

Blau does not claim his strategy is to produce a "systematic theory." Rather, he intends to offer a "theoretical prolegomenon,"[11] that is, a foundation on which theory might be built. Perhaps this qualification benefits from the hindsight available to those who write introductions to their works after the book is completed (Blau's introduction seems to fit his image); for Blau certainly does not produce theory with the effort at methodological rigor Homans attempts. However, like Homans, Blau appears to anticipate producing a fairly complete and comprehensive statement of human social behavior, a statement which, like a theory, derives its essence from universal, law-like claims grounded as they are in a wealth of empirical data. In spite of this tone of universality that permeates Blau's work,[12] he too fails at producing a complete theory. I intend to support this statement.

What is important for present considerations is Blau's claim that Homans' reductionism, even if extended into areas assumed as "given" in *Social Behavior,* would not yield an understanding of the dynamics of social structural elements.[13] Blau suggests that Homans' approach, specifically his exclusive dependence upon operant conditioning as an explanatory base, precludes any meaningful extension beyond the level of direct exchange.

PSYCHOLOGICAL UNDERPINNINGS IN HOMANS AND BLAU. In the last chapter we examined Homans' depiction of the psychological bases for social behavior. Homans is certain he can "explain" or "account for" the complexities of social behavior by utilizing a psychology (derived primarily from Pareto and Skinner) that places primary emphasis on man's constant quest for satisfaction of underlying viscerogenic and psychogenic needs. By reducing the essence of social interaction and more structured social phenomena (groups, for example) to these attempts at need satsifaction, Homans claims to have discovered the most basic of the underpinnings of society. In my comments I suggested that there are some unanswered questions in Homans' utilization of psychology that undermine the deductive chain he attempts to construct. Specifically, I suggested that the type of needs Homans deals with are *social needs* and would appear to be derivatives of man's culture and are not necessarily, as Homans appears to see them, linked to needs basic to man's physiology. The implications of this critique suggest that in his attempt to unearth "basics," Homans may, in effect, simply by depicting *the complex of conse-*

quences of an already fashioned culture on the basic psychology of man.

Blau also has trouble accepting Homans' elaboration of the psychological bases of social behavior. His primary objection is that such a beginning does not allow us to reach far enough with our explanation of society.

> To be sure, each individual's behavior is reinforced by the rewards it brings, but the psychological process of reinforcement does not suffice to explain the exchange relation that develops.[14]

While Blau questions the utility of depending solely on psychological bases for explanation, we do note his acceptance of a basic psychological element implicit in human social behavior.

> The basic social processes that govern associations among men have their roots in primitive psychological processes, such as those underlying the feelings of attraction between individuals and their desires for various kinds of rewards. These psychological tendencies are primitive only in respect to our subject matter, that is, they are taken as given without further inquiry into the motivating forces that produce them, for our concern is with the social forces that emanate from them.[15]

There are two important observations to be made about Blau's acceptance of psychological roots for basic social processes. First, we note that he takes these psychological bases as "given," claiming that he is interested only in "the social forces that emanate from them." We might compare this strategy with that of Homans. Homans' exchange model could not account for the *derivation* of complex social structures, so he took them as "given." He also took as given certain psycho-social "needs" which may in part be reducible to physiological needs, but might more legitimately be seen as derivations from culture (for example, the "need" for acceptance). Blau treats man's psychology as a "given" and in doing this, he demonstrates the same shortcomings we see in Homans. If we look at the nature of Blau's "psychology" we notice

58

similarities to those weaknesses in Homans' conceptualizations. Blau depicts as an example of his "psychological processes," the *underlying feeling of attraction* between individuals and *their desires for various kinds of rewards,* [16] where "attraction" is defined as whether an individual . . . *expects* associating with another to be in some way *rewarding* for himself, and his *interest* in the expected social rewards draws him to the other.[17]

What Blau presents as "basic psychological processes" would be better seen as *economic motives.* For we note that they involve *the expectation and calculation of personal gain* and are thus in no way reducible to "basic needs." Man is not *born* with a profit motive which induces (drives?) him to base actions on "expected social rewards;" this can only come from values and interests derived *from an already established, ongoing culture.* There is nothing "basic" to man about seeking personal gain; it must be seen as part of a cultural package presented to him as part of the gift of socialization. Blau, himself, implicitly suggests the economics in his "psychology" when he notes that social exchanges "cease when these expected reactions are not forthcoming."[18] Ekeh[19] reminds us that a theory of social exchange need not include a utilitarian economics. He notes with annoyance that Blau's "constant references" to Malinowski's *Argonauts of the Western Pacific* are confusing since Malinowski stipulated that *gain* had no place in social exchange in the Trobriands. Blau's strategy is unlike that of Malinowski and suggests an intention to resurrect the ghosts of Herbert Spencer[20] and Sir James G. Frazer,[21] both of whom premised their depiction of human society on the view that a basic utilitarianism informs the relations among men.[22]

To summarize, while both Blau and Homans recognize a psychological base for human social behavior, Blau rejects the psychology Homans adopts, claiming it is not extendable to an explanation of more complex societal phenomena, and Blau adopts as "given" a vague, undefined psychology whose manifestations (like Pareto's residues) are to be seen in the "attraction" among people mutually seeking what rewards others might give them. Blau then has quickly left behind "psychological man." The effects of this leap are to escape the here-and-now hedonism of a reinforcement theory and thus pave the way for the economics of investment planning for the future. This, Blau suggests, is the basis from which to derive the complexities of social systems.

An Intermediate Stage: The Economics of Exchange

There are three major parts to Blau's book, *Exchange and Power in Social Life*. First is Blau's tacit acceptance of a psychological basis as implicit in the elementary processes of social behavior. Next there is an identification and categorization of those economic qualities whose origin is to be found in the basic psychology of man and whose manifestations occur naturally in networks of social exchange. The third part is Blau's elaboration of the complex processes and structures whose origins are to be found in the extension of the exchange processes. I have already discussed the first of these steps and will later deal with the third; our present concern is with the intermediary stage—exchange as a reflection of an economics basic to human nature.

Like Homans, Blau sees institutionalization and related complex societal processes growing out of primary elements that are basic to direct exchange. Unlike Homans, however, Blau puts particular emphasis on the stage of emergence of an "intermediate conceptual apparatus" that will serve to connect, he claims the reality of empirical, individual exchange with the abstract conceptualizations of the grand theories of collective properties such as values, norms, organizations and institutions. The basic property of this intermediate stage is man's desire for individual self-interest profits. Blau contends that no other motives, including altruism,[23] can meaningfully account for human associations. It is man's desire for personal gain which draws him to others and provides the basis upon which he judges others to be attractive associates.[24] In his elaboration of an economic model of man Blau deals in such properties as reciprocity, maximization of profit, and diminishing marginal utility. In fact, he goes so far as to include under these imperatives not only action which is *zweck-rational* but also that which is *vertrational*.[25] However, Blau is careful to point out that his view of social exchange, even with its basis in economic motives, is different from true economic exchange. First of all, while economic exchange does not, Blau claims, typically "engender feelings of personal obligation, gratitude and trust,"[26] social exchange does. Ekeh notes that Blau's depiction of pure economic exchange is ideal-typical and does not reflect the reality of many supposed non-personal transactions which result in measures of trust or distrust.[27] There is, after all, a current vogue for protesting occasional violations of an implicit "trust" within the consumer-manufacturer relationship. *Caveat emptor* has been replaced by the indignations of consumer protest.[28]

A second distinction Blau offers between social and economic exchange is that, unlike pure economics, social exchange involves extrinsic benefits that often cannot be separated from intrinsic benefits of social association. What this means is that economic principles such as profit maximization are difficult to apply to the social sector.[29] This distinction is also open to challenge, for Blau himself admits that the detachability of extrinsic benefits from their source "is a matter of degree"[30] and in most situations does not even approach the extremes of thoroughly economic or thoroughly social exchanges.[31] Again the distinction Blau draws between these two types of exchange is not exacting enough to be accepted unchallenged.

Blau's third point is to note that in spite of the absence of binding, enforceable, contractual obligations in social exchange people usually discharge their obligations.[32] While economic exchange relies on agents *external* to the exchange (e.g., contract, agencies of enforcement) to ensure reciprocity, social exchange builds up its own *internal* sanctioning agent in the form of a *trust* or *moral obligation* to discharge responsibilities. Unlike a tradition in sociology stretching back to Durkheim, however, Blau does not see this morality as an *a priori* whose existence sui generis acts down upon the exchange. Rather, he suggests that

> social exchange relations evolve in a slow process, starting with minor transactions in which little trust is required because little risk is involved and in which both partners can prove their trustworthiness, enabling them to expand their relation and engage in major transactions. Thus, the process of social exchange leads to the trust required for it in a self-generating fashion. Indeed, creating trust seems to be a major function of social exchange, and special mechanisms exist that prolong the period of being under obligation and thereby strengthen bonds of indebtedness and trust.[33]

It is because of this perspective that Blau is able to challenge Gouldner's claim that a norm of reciprocity exists before the advent of social action and provides the context in which that action may begin.[34] Blau maintains that if such a norm exists it exists not as a "starting mechanism" for social action, rather, it serves to "reinforce and stabilize" an already existing exchange.[35] Social relations are started, Blau claims, by "the existential conditions of exchange,"[36] that is, by the realization of gain from others.

> When people are thrown together, and before common norms or goals or role expectations have crystallized among them, the advantages to be gained from entering into exchange relations furnish incentives for social interaction, thus fostering the development of a network of social relations and a rudimentary group structure.[37]

For Blau, then, exchange relations are brought about by the tenets of his economic model and only later norms and values enter. We will return to this point when we discuss the third stage of Blau's argument.

What I have suggested in the foregoing argument is that Blau's careful attempt to distinguish social exchange, as he sees it, from pure economic exchange is not all that successful. Perhaps his attempt is motivated by his proclaimed interest in mediating between individualistic and collectivist sociologies. This may help explain the ideal-typical tone of much of the distinction he draws.

In essence, the difference Blau suggests exists between social and economic exchange is that the former would appear to be enmeshed in issues of trust and morality while the latter is based on contract. We clearly see Blau wavering on this depiction of the slow, step-by-step *emergence* of a spirit of reciprocity and trust in social exchange. The fact that the "normative" quality of social exchange is *derived ad hoc* and not *given* would seem to weaken Blau's claim of differences between social and economic exchange. We are left then with a model of social exchange that closely resembles the dynamics of pure economic exchange. If there is any meaningful difference between them it probably is a matter of degree and not kind. Social exchange would seem to be somewhat "looser" than pure, contractual economic exchange. Blau notes that it involves such non-contractual items as sentiment[38] and diffused future obligations.[39] It is this looseness that allows for the derivation of other facets of exchange from the original relationship; *trust* is one of these facets, *power* is another.

POWER: THE SOCIAL BONDS OF SUPERORDINATION AND SUB-ORDINATION. Blau's primary contribution to social exchange theory is his explanation of the origin and consequences of power in social relations. While this element is implicit in the totality of our treatment of Blau, it deserves special attention.

Blau claims that social exchanges are rarely equal or even. The nature of exchange is to reflect *and* create imbalances. There are several reasons offered to support this thesis. Most obviously, exchanges may be the result of coercion; Blau, however, excludes this type of relationship from his discussion of direct exchange claiming that without choice there really is no "exchange."[40] The inequality of exchange may also be due to the principle of least interest that suggests that he who is less interested or committed to the relationship derives some advantage over the other.[41] This advantage takes the form of power when it results in compliance from the partner who places more value (interest) on the relationship.

The asymmetrical nature of direct exchange may also be a

cause of power. Blau suggests that there are some contributions which are so valuable and unilateral that they can only be repaid with some form of social deference, like the granting of esteem or status, or the granting of compliance which stipulates power of superordinates over subordinates. In this case the nature of the exchange relation itself creates differentiation of status and power. Blau notes that "the unilateral supply of important services establishes . . . credit and thus is a source of power."[42] This argument suggests Blau's primary contribution to social exchange theory, that is, that the *nature* of exchange is the *creation* of superordination and subordination through the differentiation of status and power. It is these elements which serve as the mortar, the bonds of social relations. Blau, here, clearly disagrees with Homans who stipulates balance or equality of rewards as the social bond. Homans' discussions of power (when they occur) suggest that it is an already established commodity which one brings to the exchange and then implements. Blau, on the other hand, sees power as emerging from the exchange process itself.

Blau also disagrees with the implications of Homans' use of "investments" as a basis for the evaluation of the justness of exchange, claiming that Homans uses this concept too broadly and thus "obliterates its specific meaning and its connection with justice."[43] Homans sees an exchange as just if the returns members receive from it are commensurate with their investments. Included in investments however are such things as "past histories or backgrounds."[44] In effect, Homans is suggesting a standard of justice that is based on status quo and that implicitly legitimates such inequalities of exchange as coercion, domination and exploitation.[45] All these Blau would call the exercise of *power* not justice and would claim as their origin the nature of exchange itself.

While he disagrees with Homans concerning the definitions of what is fair and just in social exchange, Blau suggests an interpretation of the possible consequences of the exercise of power that bears a close resemblance to that which he criticizes in Homans' concept of distributive justice. In order to derive this interpretation we must begin with Blau's vision of balance and imbalance in exchange.

Exchange processes are dialectical in nature.[46] What this means is that the give and take of contributions and reciprocations operates like a pendulum and results in a "strain toward imbalance . . . in social associations."[47]

> The principle suggested is that balanced social states depend on imbalances in other social states; forces that restore equilibrium in others. The processes of association . . . illustrate this princple.[48]

Exchange produces a differentiation of power through the medium of imbalance of contributions. It is not always possible to reciprocate with an equally valuable commodity; the consequences are an indebtedness by some. This indebtedness may be seen as the "power" some members have over others. Blau, here, notes a point crucial to his unique variant of social exchange theory; the exercise of power engenders different responses in different situaions—and they need not always be opposition reactions. Certainly direct coercion is "always resisted and, if possible, actively opposed"[49]—however, certain other forms of power exercised are not. Those members who perceive compliance with power to be the source of "needed benefits . . . do not necessarily experience their position as disadvantageous, although they may do so."[50] The element which, for Blau, distinguishes power opposed to "power complied with" is a "social norm of fairness"[51] (a property I will discuss later.) What Blau suggests is that there are two types of imbalance in social relations. One of these is negative for subordinates and involves "exploitation and opposition,"[52] while the other is a "positive imbalance of benefits"[53] that results in the legitimation of power as authority. Again, I propose to do a more detailed examination of these properties later; however, it is useful to note at this time that Blau's rendition of power makes it oppressive *only when it is felt as exploitive by subordinates* and this subjective evaluation depends heavily on whether the subordinate feels he is fairly "getting his money's worth" of "needed benefits." What Blau is suggesting here is quite similar to Homans' conceptualization of "distributive justice" in that power, for Blau, may often be a statement of the rightfulness of inequality in exchange.[54] While Blau's conception of power leaves its evaluation up to the subordinate's subjectivity, some Marxists might disagree and suggest that the man who sees his own subordination as "rightful" is likely suffering from "false consciousness" and is being exploited.[55]

So, unlike Homans, Blau sees the reality of differentials of power. Yet, in a way quite similar to Homans, Blau defines power and inequality as often times rightful and beneficial. In terms more familiar to Homans, Blau is in effect stipulating that "fairness" equals "rewards" minus "costs."

In conclusion we might summarize what we have so far in our elaboration of Blau's scheme. Starting with economic motives whose basis is in human psychological states uncritically accepted as given, Blau has proposed a groundwork for social exchange. The exchange process itself is premised upon operationalizing these economic motives and this leads unerringly to the exploitation of the exchange medium for power differentiations. The results of exchange then are: a differentiation of functions (approximating the "organismic" model of the 19th century); an interdependence among members which leads to integration (same organismic model); a differentiation of rank, prestige, esteem and similar properties of social groupings; and, as already mentioned, a differentiation of power.

"Power" serves as the connection with what follows. Power, when legitimated, leads to more complex and indirect processes of exchange; however, an intervening step must be introduced. Power must be judged to be rightful and for this a standard is necessary. Norms aid the extension of the properties of power into the properties of more complex levels such as organizations and institutions.

Elaboration into Macrostructures: Norms.

There are two primary levels of analysis in Blau's social exchange theory. One is the "direct exchange" of microstructures; the other is the indirect exchange of macrostructures. Most of what we have already dealt with from Blau's work applies directly to the first of these two levels. Psychological givens, the economics of exchange and the derivation and manifestation of power are all derived and elaborated in the first half of his *Exchange and Power*, the part that deals in microstructural analysis. This is not to say that these phenomena are restricted to direct exchange and cannot be applied to larger, more complex structures, but it does give us a clue that Blau, unlike Homans, does not see a smooth and causally perfect transition from microstructures to macrostructures. While these phenomena can be applied to an understanding of macrostructures, they cannot merely be transposed unaltered. Complex structure analysis involves, for Blau, some new elements for explanation mixed in with what is already suggested. We will approach Blau's argument by beginning with an examination of the two types of *trust* in his model of social behavior.

In a direct exchange between two persons we might witness the development of some properties of trust. As Blau sees it, exchanges typically begin with:

> a slow process, starting with minor transactions in which little trust is required because little risk is involved and in which both partners can prove their trustworthiness, enabling them to expand their relation and engage in major transactions.[56]

The effect of such a trial and error process is that the social exchange itself "leads to the trust required for it in a self-generating fashion."[57]

We might note two qualifications of such a conception of the origin of trust in exchange. First, this process works best in cases of restricted exchange (what Blau calls "direct exchange") for, if the participants exceed two, the delicate give and take becomes too confusing. Second, a derivation of trust, such as this, requires that each new exchange be seen as a "clear slate" with sufficient time alloted for trust to be built-up anew. Needless to say, this would be a very inefficient way to run the business of social interaction. Recognizing the limitations of such a conceptualization of trust in exchange, Blau posits the existence of another source of trust, this being an already established reservoir of a moral code, built up from the history of man's unsuccessful exchanges[58] and from which he draws a sense of *moral obligation* with which to regulate his own exchange behavior and judge that of others. Trust, then, would first appear to be an *emergent* property of exchange (and not an *a priori* whose origins are obscured), and then attains (as the result of much negotiation) a somewhat objectified status as a *general moral obligation* which each actor must assess before committing himself to an exchange. Blau is clearly attempting a reconciliation of those sociologies that challenge any view of norms as "givens" and those which begin their analysis with the already established structural consequences of process. He allows for the problematic and negotiated world of the interactionists and also draws from the fruits of functionalist analyses.

What is important in this discussion is Blau's emphasis on the distinctly different character of micro- and macro-processes. Unlike Homans, Blau attempts to have no causal link between the two, preferring to note "analogous" or "related"[59] phenomena in each. While he recognizes the emergence of complex forms from the general properties of elementary forms, he clearly stipulates that once emerged, complex phenomena such as norms and codes of obligation attain an objectivity and autonomy of their own. While Blau cautions against the oversimplification of seeing direct exchange writ large in the form of complex structures, he is consistent in his belief that economic principles underlie all of social phenomena. Even norms, which Blau recognizes as objective social facts, are not in themselves the cause of such consequences as societal integration. The norms merely provide the context in which to define and assess such direct consequences of the exchange process as power and status differentiation. It is the economics of exchange that provides the key to understanding social phenomena. And this key is premised on the assumed rationality of a world sufficiently non-problematic that the exercise of a model of economic motivation works.

There is another property of norms that permits the elaboration from micro to macro analysis. This is the ability of norms, values and related moral codes to act in an exchange relationship in place of a member of that exchange. In doing this:

> Social norms substitute indirect exchange for direct exchange transactions between individuals. The members of the group recieve group approval in exchange for conformity and the contribution to the group their conformity to social expectation makes.[60]

Blau recognizes that the direct exchange of a two person network requires more than the mere addition of "third man"[61] to effect the change into complex structures. Some new element with a broad enough reach to transcend the here-and-now of a single exchange is necessary for this extension. Norms enable exchanges to generalize such properties as time, rewards and costs. By introducing an element with the common denominator of depersonalization into individual exchanges Blau is able to account for such impersonal structures as organizations and institutions. Again, however, it is important to note that Blau, unlike Durkheim and others, does not see norms as having their source in some "higher morality;" they are nothing more than the derivatives of the economic motives of individuals.[62] Blau's treatment of Gouldner's "norm of reciprocity" as deriving from individual self-interest and *not* as "starting mechanism" of exchange is evidence for this direction.[63]

With the introduction of norms, generally held values, and indirect exchange Blau has opened the door to an examination of the complex structural properties of societies.

COMPLEX STRUCTURES SUI GENERIS. By complex structures Blau means formal organizations and institutions. Most of the second half of *Exchange and Power* deals with the derivation and operations of these phenomena.

Blau's "derivation" of complex structures is not exactly what a social scientist of the rigorous persuasion (Homans, for example) would find acceptable. Blau himself makes no claim for a deductive, causal argument: he is, after all, involved only in a "theoretical prolegomenon." While he does not claim an argument of certainty, he does suggest that "there are some parallels between the social processes in microstructures and macrostructures."[64] Reduced to its essentials Blau's claim is that both levels of social organization are explainable by referring to the same basic economic properties. There are, of course, several important differences between the two and Blau notes them.[65]

1. Whereas microstructures are held together by feelings of personal attraction, the vast numbers of people in macrostructures make attraction of a face-to-face nature impossible. The macrostructural equivalent for feelings of attraction is value consensus which serves to replace the effective ties of pairs with a more generalized, more pervasive alternative.

2. Macrostructures introduce media of exchange less personal than the emotions and attractions of microstructures; money is the most obvious of these, others might include status, honor, and "face."[66] The introduction of impersonal commodities for exchange makes it possible to "develop complex networks of indirect exchange."[67]

3. Whereas microstructures rely essentially on personal influence for control, macrostructures require a format with broader capabilities. Blau proposes that "legitimating values . . . expand the scope of centralized control far beyond the reach of personal influence."[68]

4. Macrostructures differ from microstructures in that the for-

mer are characterized by a "complex interplay" of "intricate patterns" among "diverse substructures, some of which may be microstructures, composed of individuals, while others may themselves be macrostructures composed of subgroups."[69] The consequences of this interplay include integration, differentiation, organization and opposition formation.

5. Finally, Blau notes that enduring institutions typically develop in macrostructures. The effect of this process is the development of features of transmission of values, norms, knowledge and skills from one generation to another.

We see from the foregoing that Blau, much unlike Homans, sees the development of complex structures that become sui generis, that is, they develop *objective* and *autonomous* properties separate from, but linked to, the exchange process.

While Blau does not pretend to actually "derive" these complex structures from lesser forms, he does offer an "origins" argument of some linearity. Again, we begin with the process of social attraction that, in turn, gives rise to processes of social exchange. Exchange, characterized by a tendency to be imbalanced yet with an impetus toward balance, produces differentiation of power resultant from incompletely reciprocated offerings. Power, when exercised, is judged fair or unfair according to norms of fairness and justice that members bring into play. This in turn may lead to social approval, legitimation into authority and a collective response in the form of organization, or if judged unjust may lead to collective opposition, conflict, reorganization and perhaps change. For Blau, macrostructures are said to be indirect exchanges mediated through cultural values. They attain the level of institutions when: there is a desire to formalize this indirect exchange into discernible rules; the mediating cultural values have attained sufficient regularity, habituation and objectivity so that they are internalized through processes of socialization; and the nature of such indirect exchanges is supported by such powerful and vested interests as would have them formalized. In the broadest sense, organization and institutionalization occur where legitimated power is seen as contributory to what is defined as common interests and common welfare. Here we see the most generalized representation of the unproblematic rationality implicit in Blau's economic model. For, in the end, whatever *is*, pays off and whatever does not pay off is not permitted to remain. The teleological basis of such a model of society would result in the same difficulty at explaining the existence of counterproductive organizations or outmoded institutions as would the teleology of the functionalist explanation-from-effects. How would Blau, for example, explain the existence of structures which do not contribute to common interests or welfare, yet remain unopposed? While the perspective of *qui bono* may serve well to explain the nature of the direct exchanges of microstructures; when it comes to unraveling the complexities of diverse macrostructures, it seems a too rational, unproblematic orientation. Blau does allow for a dynamic of social structure characterized by "intermittent reorganizations in a dialectical pattern"[70] as distinct from the "continuously adjusted equilibrium"[71] that may be descriptive of microstructures; however, a dialectic dealing, as it does in a mutuality of cause and effect among several elements, is not reconcilable with the rationality of an economic model that suggests uni-directionality of causation.

In the end, what we may say about Blau's analysis of complex structures is that it emphasizes that their enduring and stable nature is an outgrowth of the processes of interpersonal relations we see in direct exchange. However the jump from the lesser to the greater form is often broad and without a deductive linkage (Blau claims none) and amounts at times to a conceptual elaboration devoid of empirical foundation. Blau's concern with a social order derived from the basic economics of individual self-interest yields, on the macrostructural level, a working out of assumed rationality where such things as common values and collective perceptions of "what benefits" make the existence and reorganization of valuable complex structures an unproblematic issue.

CONCLUSION

The main sociological purpose of studying processes of face-to-face interaction is to lay the foundation for an understanding of the social structures that evolve and the emergent social forces that characterize their development.

A concern with social action, broadly conceived as any conduct that derives its impetus and meaning from social values, has characterized contemporary theory in sociology for some years. The resulting preoccupation with value orientations has diverted theoretical attention from the study of the actual associations between people and the structures of their associations. While structures of social relations are, of course, profoundly influenced by common values, these structures have a significance of their own, which is ignored if concern is exclusively with the underlying values and norms. Exchange transactions and power relations, in particular, constitute social forces that must be investigated in their own right, not merely in terms of the norms that limit and the values that reinforce them, to arrive at an understanding of the dynamics of social structures.[72]

What Blau sets out to accomplish with his theoretical prolegomenon is the establishment of a groundwork for the eventual construction of a comprehensive theory of social behavior. To do this, he first assesses the limitations of attempts that have gone before. Homans' work, while it correctly identifies the exchange medium as the basic structure and dynamic of social action cannot, Blau believes, accomplish a thorough explanation of societal phenomena because it is trapped in the mire of a reductionism that does not allow for extension to the level of complex structures. On the other hand, sociologies that stress a "value orientation" (Parsonian functionalism, for example) are capable of analyzing complex structures; however, Blau feels the nature of their approach "has diverted attention from the study of the actual associations between people and the structures of their associations"—that is, from exchange transactions and power relations.

Then Blau sets out with the intention of mediating between these theoretical extremes and hopes, thereby, to produce if not an actual deductive theory, at least the basis upon which one might later be formed. His attempts achieve some measure of success in making more exacting and broader in scope an understanding of the processes of direct exchange that Homans pursued. Blau's discovery that power results from the intrinsic asymmetry of exchange and therefore is the natural consequence of such asymmetry is perhaps his major contribution to an understanding of the dynamics of social action and its resulting structures.

Also, Blau succeeds in extending the type of systems analysis Parsons attempted so that it is, in his work, more capable of dealing with change and opposition. Blau even goes so far as to allow for a "cultural heritage" of a "counterinstitutional component."[73] His picture of society and the forces operating within it offers a portrayal of the dialectic of conflicts among diverse interests, and as such, is a more realistic (conceptually and empirically) version than Parsons' heavy reliance on the property of value consensus and the inherent stability of systems.

Blau has also managed to expand the scope of exchange theory to include elements of conflict theory, a la Marx. Blau's depiction of macrostructural change as a dialectic "that transforms simple into increasingly complex social processes and that serves as a catalyst of ubiquitous change" is as close to Marxist analysis as a self-proclaimed Durkheimian functionalist might ever go.[74] Again, the strengths of Blau's statement are results of the extent to which his theoretical offerings reflect a willingness for intellectual eclecticism. By utilizing the best aspects of several mutually exclusive perspectives Blau has managed to build a statement that goes beyond their individual limitations. If we are to heed the suggestions of Kuhn,[75] a mature science is characterized by theoretical consensus; and Blau's prolegomenon would appear to be a step in this direction.

Blau's exchange theory is not, however, without its faults. For the most part these faults are a consequence of the same theoretical "looseness" that allows Blau to include so many diverse explanations in one theoretical statement. Unfortunately, the nature of these limitations is such that it makes Blau's exchange theory unacceptable as the comprehensive statement he appears to have intended.

Blau appears to have an identity problem. In many ways he presents himself through his exchange theory as an exponent of Spencerian utilitarianism. This orientation is reflected in his heavy dependence on an economic model of self-interest which he suggests is the basic motive for human action. However, while this approach allows Blau to escape the trap of behavioral reductionism and thereby extend direct exchange into the "middle ground" of emergent power relations, it alone is unacceptable as a total explanation of more complex and enduring structures. For, if man's society were nothing more than a system of compounded self-interest it would be a fragile thing, indeed. Blau here reflects Durkheim's criticisms of Spencer in suggesting that a new, additional element is necessary for extension to macrostructures. This element is common values—or a social morality of trust. Blau suggests that the exercise of power derived from exchange is evaluated by individuals relative to an already existent norm of fairness or justice, and the result of this evaluation determines whether the collective reaction to power will manifest itself as legitimation or opposition. While Blau adroitly juxtaposes Spencerian and Durkheimian sociologies so as to "round out" his model, he minimizes, if not negates, the *irreconcilability* of these two approaches. "Self-interest" and a "greater moral code" are mutually exclusive depictions of human motives; no amount of intellectualizing will make them happy bedfellows. By resurrecting Durkheim's "morality," Blau is effectively begging the question of what happens to self-interest in the face of common interest and common welfare. Similarly, Blau offers no explanation of why a "higher morality" of fairness and justice should not totally displace the economics of self-interest on the level of direct exchange, and result, thereby, in a depiction of social action not terribly different from the "common value" orientation of Parsons. By allowing a theoretical looseness Blau has admitted all sorts of mutual enemies into his camp and is therefore thwarted in his attempt at a comprehensive explanation of social action and social structure.

Another point bears mention as to Blau's use of economic motives in exchange. By premising such a basis, Blau has implicitly denied any non-rationalistic motives for human action. Blau does mention that he is including *vertrational* as well as *zweckrational* in his model, however the nature of the determinism of seeking profit or gain in all encounters would seem to belie that claim. Blau's actor is one who theoretically should never (given that he has sufficient information) choose action which is punishing even in pursuit of an "ideal" to which he is committed. Martyrdom, for example, may be "rewarding" only in the most perverse arithmetic of rewards minus costs and is otherwise not accounted for by Blau's model.

Blau treads perilously close to sophistry when he suggests that the exercise of power that might otherwise be seen as exploitive is accepted as legitimate by subordinates when they feel they are deriving "needed benefits" through their subjugation. Blau begins his discussion of power by adopting Weber's definition of that property, but ironically minimizes what for Weber was an important distinction, that is between *Macht* (power), and *Herrschaft* (domination) over those who theoretically owe obedience. For Blau this distinction varies relative to what one derives from an exchange. To suggest that exploitation and legitimacy are definable not by objective conditions of the exchange but by the subjective interpretation given to its consequences by subordinates who may suffer the false consciousness of complacency and an ignorance of alternatives is to cloak a wolf in sheep's clothing. We need only consider Durkheim (who must have influenced much of Blau's sociology) to see a challenge to Blau's "legitimation of power." Durkheim would not consider an exchange capable of legitimation (he would call it "just") were not "the contracting parties . . . placed in conditions externally equal."[76] While Blau would offer actors' subjectively (albeit a "collective" subjectivity) as the sole determining factor in distinguishing exploitation from legitimacy, Weber, Durkheim, and, of course, Marx, would include with this a more objective basis for evaluation. As noted earlier, Blau's version of legitimated power is quite close to Homans' legitimation of the status quo in his concept, distributive justice. Blau, does not seem to have gone much further than Homans in this regard.

What Blau *has produced* is a needed elaboration of the exchange model that now allows the intricacies of a give and take of actors seeking benefits from each other and who, in doing so, manage to crystallize their relations into some variants of social structure. Granted, the model is plagued with some of the same problems we saw in Homans (Blau even adds some new ones of his own). In the larger picture, however, Blau has taken us further—toward a comprehensive theory of social action and social structure. It remains for other theorists to work with the areas of primary deficiencies in the model.

Primary among these deficiencies is the concern we note in both Homans and Blau for a social order seen as *non-problematic*—that is, the development of an *assumed rationality*. In Homans, this rationality took the form of the determinism of drives and needs; in Blau, it was represented by the motive for self-interest gain. Both of these authors, having identified what they felt was the "starting mechanism," needed only stand back as all the parts fell into place, producing a society where there had once been merely a pair of actors. Blau gives us a clue to the direction we must now seek when he states that "the assumption that men seek to adjust social conditions to achieve their ends seems to be quite realistic, indeed inescapable." Of course this is so, however Blau's own theoretical limitations are evidenced by his glossing over a most important aspect of his statement—that men *seek to adjust* social conditions." "Seeking" and "accomplishing" are not only often worlds apart but the differences between them are worthy of the most intensive study sociology can muster.

It is the pursuit of the successful application of self-interest which drives men and not the certainty of accomplishment. What we are in need of here is a sociology of pursuit, of attempt, and of the outcomes of eventualities of *failure*. We need a sociology that concerns itself with the negotiated and problematic nature of human interaction. In the next chapter we will examine the work of Erving Goffman to see if he provides this.

N O T E S

1. Richard M. Emmerson, "Operant Psychology and Exchange Theory," pp. 379-405. Also, "Exchange Theory, Part II; Exchange Relations, Exchange Networks and Groups as Exchange Systems."
2. Peter M. Blau, "Structural Effects." *American Sociological Review* 25 (1960), pp. 178-193; *Exchange and Power in Social Life,* (New York: John Wiley & Sons, 1964); "Justice in Social Exchange." *Sociological Inquiry* 34 (1964), pp. 193-206; "Interaction: Social Exchange" in David L. Sills, ed., *International Encyclopedia of the Social Sciences,* Vol. 7 (New York: Macmillan, The Free Press, 1968), pp. 452-458; "Objectives of Sociology" in Robert Bierstedt, ed., *A Design for Sociology: Scope, Objectives, and Methods* (Philadelphia: the American Academy of Political and Social Sciences, 1969), pp. 43-71.
3. Homans, puzzlingly, suggests ("Social Behavior as Exchange," p. 598), "So far as I know, the only theoretical work that makes explicit use of exchange is Marcel Mauss's *Essai sur le don.*" Why Homans would make this statement when he, himself, had attempted to unravel the exchange theory of Lévi-Strauss' work in *Marriage, Authority, and Final Causes,* is a mystery. Homans surely must have been aware of the work of Frazer and Malinowski.
4. Blau, *Exchange and Power,* p. xi.
5. Ibid., p. 3
6. Ibid., p. 13.
7. Ibid., see especially chapter 4.
8. Ibid., p. 2.
9. Homans, "A Life of Synthesis," *American Behavioral Scientist* 12 (1968), pp. 5-6.
10. Homans, *Social Behavior,* 1961, p. 51.
11. Blau, *Exchange and Power,* p. 2.
12. Blau is careful enough to note the possibility of a cultural bias in his work (see, *Exchange and Power,* pp. 6-7), however the essence of his presentation is a tone of universal applicability.
13. See Blau, "Justice in Social Exchange," p. 193.
14. Blau, *Exchange and Power,* p. 4.
15. Ibid., p. 19.

16. Ibid. (my emphasis).
17. Ibid. p. 20 (my emphasis).
18. Ibid. p. 6.
19. Ekeh, *Social Exchange Theory: The Two Traditions,* p. 169.
20. Herbert Spencer, *The Principles of Sociology* (New York and London: Appleton and Company, 1893).
21. Sir James G. Frazer, *Totemism and Exogamy: A Treatise on Certain Early Forms of Superstition and Society.* Vol. 1. (London: Dawsons of Pall Mall, 1910, 1968).
22. Blau's rendition of the utilitarian doctrine is inconsistent with his claims (see, e.g., 1960, 1969) of being a Durkheimian sociologist. Durkheim rejected Spencer's utilitarianism [see Emile Durkheim, *The Division of Labor in Society* (New York: Free Press, 1964)] because of its sole dependence on the economics of exchange. Durkheim, of course, sees a general morality serving as the mortar of social relations and not, as Spencer and Blau would suggest, personal gain.
23. Blau, *Exchange and Power,* p. 17.
24. Ibid., p. 35.
25. Ibid., p. 5.
26. Ibid., p. 94.
27. Ekeh, *Social Exchange Theory,* p. 173.
28. B. Glaser and A. Strauss (*The Discovery of Grounded Theory.* Chicago: Aldine Publ., Co., 1967, p. lin.) seem to feel that Blau deliberately sets up his model so that it has faults which, when exposed by others, will strengthen his theory.
29. Blau, 1968, p. 455.
30. Blau, 1964, p. 95.
31. Ibid.
32. Blau, "Interaction: Social Exchange," p. 454.
33. Ibid.
34. Alvin W. Gouldner, "The Norm of Reciprocity," pp. 161–179.
35. Blau, *Exchange and Power,* p. 92.
36. Ibid., p. 92.
37. Ibid., p. 92.
38. Ibid., p. 112.
39. Ibid., p. 93.
40. Ibid., p. 91.
41. Ibid., pp. 27–28.
42. Ibid., p. 22.
43. Blau, "Justice in Social Exchange," p. 195.
44. Homans, *Social Behavior,* 1961, pp. 74–75.
45. It is interesting to note that Homans' response to the many critics of this conceptualization is to rename the concept "distributive *injustice*" in his 1974 edition of *Social Behavior.*
46. See especially Blau, *Exchange and Power,* Chapter 11.
47. Ibid., p. 26.
48. Ibid., p. 26.
49. Ibid., p. 228.
50. Ibid., p. 228.
51. Ibid., p. 228.

52. Ibid., p. 30.
53. Ibid., p. 30.
54. The sociological origin of this perspective is obviously Spencerian.
55. Gouldner ("The Norm of Reciprocity") suggests that exploitation might be *objectively* determined by an "exchange of things of unequal value." I would not go this far in a direction away from Blau. To see *all* unequal exchanges as exploitive smacks of ideological paranoia.

I would suggest that Durkheim comes closest to a reasonable definition of exploitation (or "unjust exchange," as he calls it) when he sees that "The price of the object bears no relation to the trouble it cost and the services it renders," (*Division of Labor,* p. 383). Durkheim, in fact, is close to the Marxists when he suggests (ibid.) that justice in exchange depends on the fact "that the contracting parties be placed in conditions externally equal" and that there "cannot be rich and poor at birth without there being unjust contracts" (p. 384).
56. Blau, "Interaction: Social Exchange," p. 454.
57. Ibid.
58. Blau (*Exchange and Power,* p. 97) suggests that *trust* or *distrust* has the capacity, once established, to proliferate into related exchanges.
59. Ibid., p. 333.
60. Ibid., p. 259.
61. See Homans, *Social Behavior,* 1961, 1974.
62. Interestingly, if one represents Durkheim solely as the author of the *Elementary Froms of Religious Life,* trans, J. W. Swain (New York: The Free Press, 1915, 1968) this property of Blau's sociology is seen to be quite similar to Durkheim's derivation of religion. Durkheim, however, is also the author of *Suicide,* trans. Spaulding and Simpson (New York: The Free Press, 1951) and *The Division of Labor in Society,* books whose dealings with objectified phenomena are very much different from the author's earlier work.
63. Blau, *Exchange and Power,* pp. 91–92.
64. Ibid., p. 24.
65. The following are adapted from Blau, ibid., pp. 24–25.
66. See Erving Goffman's essay "On Face Work," reprinted in his *Interaction Ritual* (Chicago: Aldine, 1967), pp. 5–46.
67. Blau, *Exchange and Power,* p. 24.
68. Ibid., p. 24.
69. Ibid., p. 24.
70. Ibid., p. 11.
71. Ibid., p. 11.
72. Ibid., p. 13.
73. Ibid., p. 279.
74. Ibid., p. 314.
75. T. S. Kuhn, *The Structure of Scientific Revolutions* (Chicago: University of Chicago Press, 1962).
76. Durkheim, *The Division of Labor,* pp. 383–384.

FOUR :: *A Conspiracy of Exchange : Erving Goffman*

INTRODUCTION

I have suggested so far that the exchange model is generically most appropriate for depicting the processes of social behavior and resultant structural forms. However the two major sociological variants of this model, those of Homans and Blau, have been found to contain epistemological and methodological deficiencies that make the model incomplete and its application as a comprehensive theory tenuous. Of major consequence in a catalogue of such deficiencies is a depiction of the social arena of interaction as bound by the exigencies of schemata containing unproblematic portraits of the dynamics of human social behavior. I suggested that any theory that purports to explain or "get to" the nature of man's social behavior cannot assume explicitly or tacitly that interaction is merely the working out of the rationality of needs, biological or psychological—or of economic processes. What is lacking in such depictions is a sense of the uncertainty, problematics and negotiation we see implicit in the course of human affairs. While it is valid to imply that man's ability to *conceive* of most anything does not make it justified to say his society *will be* conceivably anything. It is to overstate the opposite when an unproblematic working out of a determinism of needs or economics is suggested as the course of human behavior. What is needed to temper the certainties of such depictions is a sociology that promotes the *pursuit of* and *attempt at* certainty, a sociology that emphasizes the problematic, "processual" nature of interaction, complete with its institutional and structural limitations and its possibilities of failure. This sociology must, however, be seen to fit the generic exchange model so as to conform to the argument that is presented here: exchange is the basic medium of social behavior.

In two decades, Erving Goffman has produced a sociology (or social psychology—the distinction here is quite arbitrary) that has energized many older and newer sociologists with a concern for the phenomenology of everyday life. He has imparted a sociological perspective on social behavior that emphasizes the uncertainty and problematic nature of such activity and the means by which actors attempt to shore up the perpetual jeopardy of their existential condition. In this chapter we will examine the corpus of Goffman's work with an eye toward his contributions to a realistic and epistemologically defensible portrayal of the human condition. Specifically, we will be concerned with Goffman's analysis of everyday face-to-face behavior as it fills in voids so far disclosed in the exchange model. Goffman will be pictured as a sociologist who identifies the real-life contingencies of interaction and in whose sociology is to be found some of those elements needed to round out the exchange model.

I also suggest in what follows that Goffman has written two sociologies. One is most formally articulated in his *The Presentation of Self in Everyday Life*[1] and is elaborated in some earlier papers and a number of later works.[2] It is this line in Goffman's writings that concentrates on the dynamic and structural details of face-to-face behavior as phenomena in and of themselves. Here Goffman has displayed a genius for observation and a sensitivity for the nuances of delicate balances and imbalances between actors' performances.[3]

The second line in Goffman's writings is primarily depicted in *Asylums* and also "Mental Symptoms and Public Order."[4] Here Goffman adds to his unique ability at observing the individual as interactant amid other actors, a sense of the confrontation between the individual and the institutionalized and structural aspects of society. We will suggest that these two lines or directions typify the strengths and weaknesses of Goffman's sociology. While he excels perhaps beyond comparison with anyone else at dealing with the actor *qua* actor, his primary weakness is that he has not fully developed a structural, institutional sociology to complement his analysis of face-to-face behavior. Such a direction is begun in *Asylums* but is quickly left behind for the continuation of an interactive model.

SOURCES AND ELABORATIONS

Goffman's writings reflect the coming together of several distinct and often contradictory sociological traditions. In itself this is ample cause for discovering mysteries, incongruities and multiple directions in an author's work. Goffman, however, adds another measure of complication by presenting a rendition of the fruit of these juxtapositions in such a unique and idiosyncratic way as to make the unraveling even more difficult. Goffman's use of language makes him one of the most intelligible of writers of sociology yet his penchant for obscure references and a plethora of anecdotal illustrations makes the reading of his works often an exercise in confronting obfuscation. For the amount of sociology he has written he offers a relative dearth of references to classical and contemporary "conventional" sociologists, preferring to cite as illustrative and supportive materials such items as one would find in a 19th century book of manners, or a primer for espionage, intelligence and guerrilla warfare. Certainly these idiosyncracies are defensible when one understands the nature of Goffman's particular frames of reference for everyday social behavior; however, they make it more difficult to trace the intellectual origins of his work in sociology.

In what follows, I will attempt such a trace and will suggest that Goffman's directions are understandable by referring to a few major and, for the most part, traditional sources.

This will not merely be an historical sketch; I will, in addition to identifying sources, suggest what Goffman has made of their heritages. This discussion will culminate in a statement of synthesis that first suggests something about the way Goffman views the social scene; second, that will offer the beginnings of the theme to be developed in this chapter—that is, that Goffman's sociology represents an important addition and corrective to the exchange model in that he sees man's society as the result of a problematic process of the mutual exchange of appearances and support.

The Dramaturgical Perspective

Goffman conceives of social behavior as "performances" among "actors" who adjust as best they can the "expressions" they "give" and "give off" so as to convey the "impression" that they are what they claim to be. This is done in "front" regions where the actor is in the presence of an "audience" of others who are attuned to viewing the performance as authentic or unauthentic, sincere or insincere, believable or not believable. Actors "prepare" their performances in "back" regions where they are typically not "on" and where they are able to anticipate the chances of pleasing or not pleasing the audience. However, when they are "on," actors are generally aware that audiences expect a coherence "among settings, appearance and manner"[5] that will contribute to a general willingness to "tactfully" accept the appearances of others. In all this, interactions are seen as fragile, delicate things that "can be shattered by very minor mishaps,"[6] such as "unmeant gestures or faux pas"[7] and which often require certain "techniques" of performance to sustain them.

This perspective that Goffman terms "dramaturgy"[8] is drawn primarily from the writings of the literary critic, Kenneth Burke,[9] and the phenomenologist, Gustav Ichheiser.[10]

Ichheiser's paper is derived from a number of his earlier works (most of them were published in European journals) and represents a phenomenological attempt at analyzing distortion in social perception. He deals with the everyday discrepancies between reality and appearances and suggests that "actors" and "spectators" are involved in the giving and receiving of "impressions" and "expressions."[10] The latter he defines as "symbolic relations between the external characteristics and the way they impress the observer or the way the observer responds to them."[11] The point of all this is to approach interaction and its communicative concomitant as problematic states of human affairs. Ichheiser notes that Cooley's "looking-glass-self" conceptualization made an important advance in this direction but was, unfortunately, never deeply enough explored. Ichheiser sets out to detail the "how" of the process Cooley pointed to, attempting as he does to get closer to an understanding of the *processes* involved in human relations of the micro-social order. In addition to involving a primitive form of a dramatistic ontology in the sense of identifying individuals *as* "actors" and "spectators," Ichheiser places primary emphasis on the "situation" as crucial and largely determinative for role performance and identity. Goffman, who cites Ichheiser's paper in his own *Presentation of Self* appears to have come to many the same directions either by way of Ichheiser, or by paralleling him.[12]

There are two important points made in Ichheiser's phenomenological statement that, ironically, Goffman does not handle in any depth (when he does at all) and which have been noted as important criticisms of his dramaturgy. First is Ichheiser's suggestion that a dramatic metaphor (or ontology) makes evident the "sociological roots" of schizoid personality formation.[13] Here Ichheiser posits the inevitable conflict between the "essential" self and the role self. Goffman, on the other hand, is often criticized for constructing a model of the self that all too easily allows for a facility for "distancing from" and situationalizing of ethics and thus promotes the presentation of unauthenticity and the resulting identity turmoil experienced by the individual.[14]

The second point touched on by Ichheiser is the link between the evolution of a performance ethic and the condition of alienation, both personal and as a cultural malaise. Goffman's sociology neatly depicts the functional unauthenticity of men who wear masks but he seldom approaches the historical bases for the derivation of such an adaptation to social life. Ichheiser pointed out in 1949 (perhaps earlier in foreign publications) what Urbanek more recently (and more fully) elaborated.[15] Urbanek suggests:

> To describe the alienated world as a performance only, and all the people as actors, without any analysis of how it happens that the world is a theater, a stage with historically determined actors, and what the reduction of man to a mask and role means, is insufficient.[16]

Urbanek claims that Marx's concepts of alienation and reification of human relations should be the historical and social groundings of the dramaturgical perspective. For, man, living in an alienative, reified world (i.e., capitalism) has no recourse but to become unauthentic because the authenticity of his essential self or "species-being" has been taken from him.

> Men are not authentic individualities, but are forced to put on masks. Under the pressure of particular conditions their individual characters are suppressed to such a degree that they mostly have a socially shared, impressed character, and therefore one which is also alien and not their own. For this reason, Marx's conception is also the conception of the individual, of personality, and as such includes the social psychological aspect.[17]

Again, Goffman pays little attention to such an historical grounding, preferring to deal solely with the everyday consequences of such effects.

Above any other source, Goffman's sociology owes its greatest debt to the work of Kenneth Burke. In the 1930s, Burke developed what he called a "dramatistic model" of human behavior.[18] Essentially Burke suggested that human behavior and the meanings that are given to such behavior are neither "fixed" nor are they to be seen as "absolute." Behavior is action and, as such, is not approachable by recourse to determinative organismic notions of equilibrium or homeostasis or by reference to external environments and singular processes of adaptation. Rather behavior is to be treated as "dramatistic," a process of people relating to each other *as* actors (not "as if" actors).[19]

In addition to an orientation to action, Burke details the symbolic nature of human communication and interpretation as it constitutes actors' meaning-endowing processes.

> Stimuli do not possess an *absolute* meaning. Even a set of signs indicating the likelihood of death by torture has another meaning in the orientation of a comfort-loving skeptic than it would for the ascetic whose worldview promised eternal reward for martyrdom. Any given situation derives its character from the entire framework of interpretation by which we judge it. And differences in our ways of sizing up an objective situation are expressed subjectively as differences in our assignment of motive.[20]

Thus, meaning is not a characteristic of the world. It is the result of process—an evolving, social process with others. This emphasizes the nature of meaning as *problematic* and not as an objective given. Likewise, the self (of self-identity) is not a given but is derived through the continuous process of activity—its own and that of others toward it. The self, thus, is not a certain, essential thing but is *situational,* the *result of*, not the beginnings of, interactions. As Burke said, "Doing is being," and the implication, of course, is that different "doings" result in self and other perceptions of different "beings." Berger notes similarly that:

> Roles carry with them both certain actions and the emotions and attitudes that belong to these actions. The professor putting on an act that pretends to wisdom comes to feel wise.[21]

...identity is socially bestowed, socially sustained and socially transformed.[22]

As with meaning and self, the reasons or "motives" we give to our acts are, Burke feels, not "real" but are situational rationalizations.

> I am merely attempting to suggest that a terminology of motives is not evasive or self-deceptive, *but is moulded* to fit our general orientation as to purposes, instrumentalities, the "good life."[23]

Motives, ordinarily the "whys" of behavior, are approached in Burke's schema as activity to be looked at phenomenologically in terms of "hows." Motives are "work" and are not approachable by a science that looks to antecedent knowledge as determinative of action. To fully apprehend motive, Burke tells us that we must see it as an element of the situation and not as something "inside" man to be carried from situation to situation. Motives are products of communication, evolving out of the same process as does the self. We expect actors then to attempt to be consistent in their identities and their motives; we expect congruence between act and meaning. In all, we expect actors to have prepared well enough so as to be *convincing*.

Methodologically, there are at least two areas in which the dramatistic perspective differs from the sociologies we previously examined. First, the aim of dramatism (and Goffman's dramaturgy) is to *describe* (not *explain*) interaction and its related processes. Since this is the case we will not expect to find the rigor of an attempt at explanation (such as Homans'). We will not find causal propositions or attempts to link together a litany of the present act, the past condition or "future eventuality." Rather we will see a singular devotion to the details of the situation. For Burke, this involved five key elements: scene, agent, act, agency and purpose, all of these restricted to the act at hand.[24]

The second methodological uniqueness is the treatment in terms accorded to the elements in human social action. Since dramatistic models reject traditional notions of what is "behind" social behavior, we will not see discussions of drives or drive-states, of needs, of cognitive underpinnings. Actors are "real" in terms of their activity with others in specific situations; whatever is not discernible as a part of those situations is outside of dramatistic interest. Similarly, larger structures and institutions typically are not represented in situation analysis (other than the interpretation actors "give" to their existence). The primary purpose for structure is to provide a "frame"[25] in which action takes place. Actions *define* situations; situations come to be defined by the *activity* of the situation and not by imposing finite absolutes of meaning beforehand. Of course, this does not imply that structural conditions do not impose objective conditions on interaction. However, it is important to note that regardless of their "objectivity," these conditions are open to the situational process of negotiating essences and meanings. Prison is an objective facticity that cannot be ignored: for the guilty who seek social absolution through penitence, however, it might seem if not pleasurable, then perhaps tolerable.

It should be noted that Burke and Goffman are not alike in all aspects of their individual variants on the dramatic model: Burke writes as a philosopher and a literary critic and Goffman writes as an ethnographer and social psychologist. One is concerned more with details of a method for analysis; the other builds the empirical basis for a social psychology. This difference results in a different orientation toward the universality of application of the dramatic model. For Burke, dramatism would appear to have almost universal application.

> We wish simply to emphasize the fact that, insofar as the neurological structure remains a constant, *there will be a corresponding constancy in the devices by which society is maintained.* Changes in the environmental structure will, of course, call forth changes in the peculiarities of rationalization...*But the essentials of purpose and gratification will not change.*[26]

And, in introducing *A Grammar of Motives*, Burke claims to be "concerned with the basic forms of thought which, in accordance with the nature of the world *as all men necessarily experience it* are exemplified in the attributing of motives."[27]

Goffman's approach to universal application is interesting. His studies are replete with examples and anecdotes drawn from many cultures, yet he disclaims any necessary applicability of the dramaturgical method to cultures other than our own or even to all of our culture.

> I did not mean to imply that the framework presented here is culture-free or applicable in the same areas of social life in non-Western societies as in our own....We must not overlook areas of life in other societies in which other rules are apparently followed.[28]

> Furthermore, we must be very cautious in any effort to characterize our own society as a whole with respect to dramaturgical practices.[29]

We see that while Goffman and Burke agree on the fact that communication is never context-free, Goffman is more cautious when it comes to claiming universality.[30] Goffman would appear to be more sensitized to the socio-cultural patterning of communication in his caveat that we must know the *group* in order to know the *rules* it employs in communication.

A final word is necessary that regards a point made earlier: it was suggested that Burke and Goffman differ with respect to the application of the dramatic model as metaphor or ontology; Goffman adopts the former while Burke represents the latter orientation. For Goffman the use of dramaturgy as metaphor does not suggest that men are "acting" in the sense that this is implied in Burke—rather it claims to "see more clearly" the acting by seeing men "as if" they were actors.[31] It is important to note here that Goffman's emphasis is on a *sense* of reality among those we would see as actors. "The important thing about reality," he claims, "is our sense of its realness..."

With the heritage from Ichheiser and Burke we see that Goffman has brought into play the problematic-interactive nature of man's behavior, self and cognitive apparatus. Social behavior is to be treated as drama where actors demonstrate their authenticity by performance capability and where their performance is ever in jeopardy. "Life may not be much of a gamble, but interaction is."[32] We are constantly in danger of our act suffering from some untoward intrusion that will disallow the self we are attempting. In the end, we *owe* it to ourselves and to those around us who benefit from our competences to "be the sort of person who is practiced in the ways of the stage."[33]

Self and Situation

Goffman's sociology owes much to the development of a social conception of *self*, as in the work of George Herbert Mead.[34] Mead suggests that the self "must be accounted for in terms of the social process, and in terms of communication.[35] In so doing he implicitly proclaims the primacy of the act and the situation over the individual mind or self; for, "mind arises through communication by a conversation of gestures in a social process or context of experience..."[36] The self, then, is born, nurtured and renewed in the context of social experience. It is not an essential quality born out of nothingness and then brought all packaged to each situation.

Mead suggests a duality inherent in the self; he terms its two parts: "I" and "me." The "I" is the spontaneous, impulsive, unselfconscious aspect of the self—the part capable of creativity and expression of biological drives. It is (in a somewhat perverse way) the expression of autonomy and human freedom; yet, ironically, because it cannot be apprehended by present consciousness and "appears only in memory" its appreciation is always retrospective.[37] As impulse, the "I" has the capacity for "uncontrolled conduct" and as such requires an inhibiting agent.[38] This is in the form of the second part of the self—the "me." The "me" is the sum of a history of social responses to the expressions of the "I." It is the truly "social" aspects of self and acts as a "censor" for the "I."[39] The "me" is built up experientially and thus reflects the contexts from which it emerges (a condition reminiscent of

Burke's "doing is being" dictum). While the "I" is in many ways rooted in the biology of the individual (Mead, in fact, calls it the "biologic I"), the "me" is thoroughly a product of society.[40]

Mead posits a dialectic between the "I" and the "me." One is ever-striving for unfettered expression while the other is committed to containing this expression and making it appear within the proprieties of society. This result is a continuous tension of reach and resistance which pits the animal against the values of the group. While the existence of the "I" component of self suggests that man will never be thoroughly socialized,[41] Mead's position is that it is sufficiently contained (as long as the "stress" does not become "too great") so that society is possible.[42]

The "me" makes possible self-reflection. Only through it can we apprehend ourselves as "objects," realizing self-consciousness. This capability makes possible self-assessment (crucial for *any* "actor") and the capacity for reason and the assessment of self among a network of other selves. In this way, we are capable of effecting, controlling, guiding and maneuvering ourselves while taking account of others and the specific contexts in which we interact. This dynamic capability is essential for the development of any scheme that presents man as an actor, on stage—and among other actors because it allows for the capacity for a *multiplicity* of selves, each attuned to a new situation.

Goffman reflects Mead's legacy when he claims:

> The expressive coherence that is required in performances points out a crucial discrepancy between our all-too-human selves and our socialized selves. As human beings we are presumably creatures of variable impulse with moods and energies that change from one moment to the next. As characters put on for an audience, however, we must not be subject to ups and downs....A certain bureaucratization of the spirit is expected so that we can be relied upon to give a perfectly homogeneous performance at every appointed time.[43]

> Through social discipline, then a mask of manner can be held in place from within.[44]

Here Goffman is clearly positing the self-same inner tension between the "all-too-human selves" and the "socialized selves" that Mead saw between the "I" and the "me." In addition to this situation of the duality of self and its resultant tension, Goffman closely parallels or draws from Mead on several other points.

With Mead and Goffman, the self is situational—born out of the context of interaction and reflective of the social exigencies of situation. In this, both claim the primacy of the act over most qualities that individuals bring to action, suggesting that it is in the act that both meaning and self are established. While Mead identifies as the impulsive and potentially uncontrolled entity of self that part he terms the "I," Goffman alludes to this same impulsiveness and uncertainty by portraying the potential flaws in the actor's performance that contribute to a bad showing. So, the actor can "forget himself" and "blurt out a relatively unperformed exclamation,"[45] or "create a scene" by "inopportune intrusions,"[46] or even "flood out" an uncontrolled and embarassing expression-out-of-character. Or, as with Mead's "me," the actor might be capable of manifesting "self control" and "suppress his emotional response to his private problems,"[47] or have sufficient "presence of mind" to "cover up on the spur of the moment for inappropriate behavior,"[48] thus "suppress[ing] his spontaneous feelings."[49] It should appear obvious that even in his use of terms (e.g., "self control," "presence of mind") Goffman reflects the Meadian legacy.

As with Mead, Goffman would have us see the individual as having a multiplicity of selves, each a response to a different situation with different others and different exigencies. Often the weight of these manifold demands on our identities forces us to "distance" ourselves from some of these situations and the performances they require. "Role distance" is the term Goffman uses for this behavior,[50] and he claims that it is a typical response to a normative situation.

We see that the individual limits the degree to which he embraces a situated role, or is required to embrace it, because of society's understanding of him as a multiple-role-performer rather than as a person with a particular role.[51]

...role distance can...be seen as a response to a normative framework.[52]

In all, we see in Goffman the dynamic of a presentation of self which is resultant, first of all, from the duality and inner tension Mead posits between an autonomous self and a social self—one responsive to the impulsive nature of the animal and the other necessarily derived from a history of performances to others which have, as with most past performances, already been reviewed. It is the need to ever-perfect the performance that leads man to behave "as if" he were an actor on a stage.

The second basis for such a performance motif is the crucial and determinitive quality of "place"—the situation, the role or the frame.

Social situations at least in our society, constitute a reality *sui generis*....[53]

The individual comes to doings as someone of particular biographical identity even while he appears in the trappings of a particular social role. The manner in which the role is performed will allow for some "expression" of personal identity, of matters that can be attributed to something that is more embracing and enduring than the current role performance and even the role itself, something, in short, that is characteristic not of the role but of the person—his personality, his perduring moral character, his animal nature, and so forth. However, this license of departure from prescribed role is itself something that varies quite remarkably, depending on the "formality" of the occasion, the laminations that are being sustained, and the dissociation currently fashionable between the figure that is projected and the human engine which animates it. *There is a relation between persons and role. But the relationship answers to the interactive system—to the frame—in which the role is performed and the self of the performer is glimpsed. Self, then, is not an entity half-concealed behind events, but a changeable formula for managing oneself during them. Just as the current situation prescribes the official guise behind which we will conceal ourselves, so it provides for where and how we will show through, the culture, itself prescribing what sort of entity we must believe ourselves to be in order to have something to show through in this manner.* [54]

For Goffman, as with Mead, the act, the context and the situation weigh heavily in the determination of the self that is presented to others. Goffman strongly suggests this in *Frame Analysis* where he grapples with the conflict between an orientation toward the negotiability of reality implied in Thomas's "definition of the situation" and a more determinative situation-priority perspective. Of course, the situation-dominant direction dominates.

> Defining situations as real certainly has consequences, but these may contribute very marginally to the events in progress...Presumably a 'definition of the situation' is almost always to be found, but those who are in the situation ordinarily do not *create* this definition, even though their society often can be said to do so; ordinarily, all they do is to assess correctly what the situation ought to be for them and then act accordingly. True, we personally negotiate aspects of all the arrangements under which we live, but often once these are negotiated, we continue on mechanically as though the matter had always been settled. [55]

> I personally hold society to be first in every way and any individual's current involvement to be second.... [56]

> Not, then, men and their moments. Rather moments and their men. [57]

The Functions and Dynamics of Ritual and Secular Morality

A third and very important exemplar for Goffman's writings is the sociology of Emile Durkheim. Specifically, it is with Durkheim that we find the roots of two concepts basic to Goffman's work—the functions of ritual and a secular morality.

To understand what Goffman derives from Durkheim, it is necessary to outline carefully some of the essentials of Durkheim's work. He is one of the most misinterpreted of the early sociologists and an improper rendition of his ideas would only serve to confuse our understanding of how Goffman handles them. Among classical sociologists who are in most danger of being misread and oversimplified are the ones whose sociology is driven by a passion for finding a corrective to social problems. The nature of attempting amelioration is such that both the author and the reader often tend to overemphasize elements of an argument to accentuate its urgency. Much of Durkheim's sociology is intended as a corrective;[58] therefore, perhaps, we should not be surprised at the way he is often portrayed in simplistic, overly-dichotomized terms. The "social determinist" who "neglects" the individual while extolling the "power" and "fact-like" nature of society—this, often, is the reading that Durkheim's writings get. To properly understand the complexity of Durkheim's contribution to sociology and the particular manner in which he is utilized in the present argument it is necessary to unravel the basic themes of his writings from the overly-dichotomized reading they often obtain.

Durkheim's works, as much as any important author in the formative period of sociological thought, are a product of the intellectual milieu in which they occur. Nisbet sees Durkheim's concerns in sociology as a consequence of a society still under the effects of "two great revolutions of modern times—the industrial revolution and the political revolution."[59] Durkheim was also involved in an attempt to refute the impact of a third revolution, a democratic one, which accentuated the basic Cartesian dualism of man the individual, and society as merely his derivative. Durkheim saw this over-accentuation of individualism reflected in the new field of psychology, and in the utilitarian doctrine of Spencer, among others.[60] Durkheim's concerns dealt with a society whose binding communal qualities he saw eroding with the impact of a rapidly evolving modern industrialism and hyper-individualism. The potentials he saw were destructive both for society and the individual: social decay, moral decay, excessive egoism, *anomie*. These were to be the legacies of the rapid progress of the past century. Durkheim's response to this vision was anything but simplistic. He did not propose a corrective "religion" of sociology nor did he advocate vast sweeping reform. However, he did, grapple with what should be seen as a theme basic to all of his major writings—that is, the duality of "individual man," with his potential for excessive egoism and "social man" whose strengths lie in the elevation to a level higher than himself of the cohesive and "sacred" qualities of society.

> There are two beings in him: an individual being which has its foundation in the organsim and the circle of whose activities is therefore strictly limited, and a social being which represents the highest reality in the intellectual and moral order that we can know by observation—I mean society.[61]

For Durkheim this duality must be resolved in favor of "social man"; only through the primacy of society can the malaise of modern man be rectified and his authentic individualism obtained.

> Social man necessarily presupposes a society which he expresses and serves. If this dissolves, if we no longer feel it in existence and action about and above us, whatever is social in us is deprived of all objective foundation. All that remains is an artificial combination of illusory images, a phantasmagoria vanishing at the least reflection; that is, nothing which can be a goal for our action. Yet this social man is the essence of civilized man; he is the masterpiece of existence. Thus, we are bereft of reasons for existence, for the only life to which we could cling no longer corresponds to anything actual, the only existence still based upon reality no longer meets our needs.[62]

The complexity of Durkheim's vision is that his emphasis on society, as opposed to the individual, causes him to be interpreted as reflecting a reified conception of man's world; that is, his sociology often "appears" to lose sight of the *man-process* of society's objectification. For example, Durkheim's view of society is that it is not a "mere sum of individuals." Rather, the system formed by their association represents a specific reality that has its own characteristics."[63] Durkheim, however, is not reifying society; rather, he is indicating that it should be investigated *as it is seen to be real by its members*. Evidence for this is to be found in Durkheim's classic discussion of "social facts."[64] "Consider social facts as things," Durkheim tells us.[65] By this famous admonition he is *not* claiming an ontology of social facts; rather, he is indicating an epistemological concern for a developing science of sociology that must deal with the institutional world in the sense in which it is objectified human activity. In other words, social facts represent the externalization and objectification of man-work; to comprehend the society in which man exists we must see it as he sees it—as things. So, for example, when Durkheim discusses "law" as "materialized so as to become an element of the external world," he has not lost sight of the fact that while law is external to and coercive of men it is also the embodiment of man-work.[66] "Law" may be "materialized" but "coerciveness" is not; it remains a property of the mind—not any less potent, but real insofar as men experience it as real.

> One can, indeed, without distorting the meaning of this expression, designate as "institutions" all the beliefs and all the modes of conduct *instituted* by the collectivity. Sociology can then be defined as the science of institutions, of their genesis and of their functioning.[67]

Durkheim's epistemological, rather than ontological, intent is clarified in his response to critics of the first edition of *Rules:*

> The proposition which states that social facts are to be treated as things...is one of those which have provoked most contradiction...we assert not that social facts are material things but that they are things by the same right as material things....
> What precisely, is a "thing?" A thing differs from an idea in the same way as that which we know from without differs from that which we know from within. Things include all objects of knowledge that cannot be conceived by purely mental activity, those that require for their conception data from outside the mind, from observations and experiments, those which are built up from the more external

and immediately accessible characteristics to the less visible and more profound. *To treat the facts of a certain order as things is not, then, to place them in a certain category of reality but to assume a certain mental attitude toward them...*[68]

Durkheim continues, indicating quite explicitly both his methodological intent and his conception of the man-process basis of social facts:

> Such a procedure an "objective study" is all the more necessary with social facts, for consciousness is even more helpless in knowing them than in knowing its own life. The objection will be raised that, since *social facts are our own personal constructs*, we have only to resort to introspection in order to determine *what we put into them and how we formed them*. But we must remember that the greater part of our social institutions was bequeathed to us by former generations....How, then, should we have the faculty of discerning with greater clarity the causes, otherwise complex, from which collective acts proceed? For, at the very least, each one of us participates in them only as an infinitesimal unit; we have a multitude of collaborators, and what takes place in other consciousnesses escapes us.
>
> Our principle, then implies no metaphysical conception, no speculation about the fundamental nature of beings. What it demands is that the sociologist put himself in the same state of mind as the physicist, chemist, or physiologist when he probes into a still unexplored region of the scientific domain.[69]

Then we come to a recognition of the complex quality of Durkheim's conceptualization of man and society. Society is man, externalized and objectified. In a manner quite similar to Marx, Durkheim has pointed to the thing-like quality obtained by "our own personal constructs." But this is only one half of the dialectic; the other half is the determination of the quality of man *by* society and social forces. Perhaps in this area Durkheim makes his most distinctive contribution.

To understand the importance of this theme for Durkheim, we must remind ourselves of his deep concern for what he saw as the potential for moral decay of social integration and the resultant effects upon the individual—egoism and anomie. For

Durkheim, society, when it works properly, *is* morality; only through the association of man with man is morality realized. "Man is a moral being only because he lives in society, since morality consists in being solidary with a group."[70] In *The Division of Labor in Society*, Durkheim traces the development of society from a "mechanical" form of solidarity where traditional moral beliefs are the cement of a society of "sameness," to "organic" solidarity where the contractual nature of an extended "division of labor" and delocalization of the individual from family, native soil and traditions force a loosening of traditional values and morality and require an alternative form of stability. Durkheim sees a general moral nature that grows out of the very diffuseness of organic society. A morality which derives from man's externalized and objectivated activity so that it confronts him as a facticity with a self-contained imperative to morality.

> Thus, it is wrong to oppose a society which comes from a community of beliefs to one which has a cooperative basis, according only to the first a moral character, and seeing in the latter only an economic grouping. In reality, cooperation also has its intrinsic morality. There is, however, reason to believe...that in contemporary societies this morality has not yet reached the high development which would now seem necessary to it.[71]

Durkheim's general perspective is that the strength of the "collective conscience" (the "likeness" of adherence to a traditional moral order) varies inversely with individuality or egoism.[72] Similarly, collective conscience declines with organic solidarity—however, it does not disappear. Through a particular form of moral individualism (a "cult of the individual"),[73] an accentuation of the worth and dignity of the individual in a cooperative system provides for a morally integrated division of labor. While amoral individualism can in the extreme lead to moral anomie, Durkheim's vision is that individualism in modern society is not fully amoral. Durkheim expresses this concept in his portrayal of freedom. "To be free is not to do what one pleases; it is to be master of oneself."[74]

Freedom, for Durkheim, is the perfection of oneself as a member of society.[75] To achieve this perfection the individual must submit to society; only through "regulation" and "social rules" can personal liberty be achieved,[76] for "only a constituted society enjoys the moral and material supremacy indispensable in making law for individuals....It alone has continuity and the necessary perpetuity to maintain the rule."[77] The value of the state is its ability to become a "moral control," replacing the loss of traditional bonds that occurred with the increase in individual freedom of modern society.[78] Durkheim's dialectic, then, is the recognition of both the man-constituted nature of society and the direction society imposes on man in its constituted form. To complete the dialectic man subsumes himself to society as the Socratic student to teacher, thus sitting at the feet of the source of knowledge. Society "requires that, forgetful of our own interest, we make ourselves its servitors, and it submits us to every sort of inconvenience, privation and sacrifice, without which social life would be impossible."[79] Anomie can then be seen as a breakdown of the dialectic. The individual is no longer protected by the potency of objectified "knowledge"—he is adrift from society and from the source of all knowledge. Durkheim's freedom, then, is a freedom *to choose not to be totally free*. To be totally free is to suffer from the weakness inherent in hyper-individualism. Only a "moral" individualism satisfies *both* society and the individual.[80]

While Durkheim's primary emphasis is undoubtedly on the effect society has on the individual, he allows the individual to be less than a captive—conscious of a constraining and coercive process. Durkheim's sociology provides for the process of *internalization*,[81] that is, the assimilation of objective social facts so that they become subjectively meaningful as individual desires.

There are at least two levels at which *internalization* occurs and the individual is, thus, divested of the "weight" of external constraint: (1) his belief in the "existence" of a "moral authority"[82] and (2) his perception of himself as an individual.

1. The constraining nature of society is, according to Durk-

heim, not ordinarily made explicit nor perceived[83] because the individual typically accepts the legitimacy of his obligation to a duly constituted moral order.[84]

> If rules whose violation is punished do not need a juridical expression, it is because they are the object of no contest, because everybody feels they are the object of no contest, because everybody feels their authority.[85]

And, in speaking of the mechanism by which the collective conscience and collective sentiments are implemented, Durkheim writes:

> Not only are they engraven in all conscience, but they are strongly engraven. They are not hesitant and superficial desires, but emotions and tendencies which are strongly ingrained in us.[86]

2. The second level of internalization reflects society's unique ability to achieve compliance while allowing the individual to perceive himself as an individual without feelings of servitude. Again, speaking of social facts, Durkheim notes:

> Because beliefs and social practices thus come to us from without, it does not follow that we receive them passively or without modification. In reflecting on collective institutions and assimilating them for ourselves, *we individualize them and impart to them more or less personal characteristics.* Similarly, in reflecting on the physical world, *each of us colors it after his own fashion*, and different individuals adapt themselves differently to the same physical environment. It is for this reason that *each one of us creates, in a measure, his own morality, religion, and mode of life.* There is no conformity to social convention that does not comprise an entire range of individual shades. It is nonetheless true that this field of variations is a limited one. It verges on nonexistence or is very restricted in that circle of religious and moral affairs where deviation easily becomes crime. It is wider in all that concerns economic life. But, sooner, or later, even in the latter instance, one encounters the limit that cannot be crossed.[87]

So, while Durkheim posits the primacy of society, he recognizes that its powers can only be actualized through the cooperation of its members. Of the collective conscience Durkheim writes, "It is...an entirely different thing from particular consciences, although it can be realized only through them."[88] In the sense in which George Herbert Mead distinguished an "object," as the result of action, the "character and meaning" the individual assigns to a stimulus,[89] so the individual gives society its "objectified" and "real" nature. Throughout, man is seen as the constitutor of that reality.

Mediating between man and society in this process is activity that Durkheim sees as ritualistic.[90] Social rituals, Durkheim claims, are the primary processes sustaining social values. It is through the ritualized solidarity which we see in ceremony that constructions of morality are renewed and perpetuated and from which man derives his most basic conceptions of reality. Durkheim traces ritual from primitive societies where it serves to unite men with the gods they create and that come to represent their social organization, to organic societies with their high degree of division of labor where ritual is secularized to reflect the collective identity of man. In this later stage ritual becomes the framework for relations between men rather than between men and gods.

For Durkheim, ritual in both primitive and more developed social orders is a consequence of several factors coming together: physical co-presence; the desire to coordinate common behavior; and, the directing of a collective focus on an object or objects common to the interests of all. When these three conditions have been met, men ritualize much of their lives, forming an important link in the chain between man and the social order.

Goffman's sociology is an overall reflection of the concerns and directions of the corpus of Durkheim's work. In the most general sense Goffman's writings reflect Durkheim's concern for the eroding of binding communal qualities. As in Durkheim's era, Goffman's society is characterized by rapid changes in technology and social patterns. The consequences of these sorts of changes were reflected in Durkheim's focus on the anomic potential for men who are left with fewer traditional patterns and gods to cleave to. Goffman echoes this vision by displaying modern man adrift from old moorings and worshipping the new secular gods of appearance and impression complete with their own variations of devotional rituals.

Goffman reflects the "moral decay" that Durkheim envisioned by portraying modern man as essentially amoral. As performers, according to Goffman:

> Individuals are not concerned with the moral issue of realizing...standards, but with the amoral issue of engineering a convincing impression that these standards are being realized. Our activity, then, is largely concerned with moral matters, but as performers we do not have a moral concern in these moral matters. As performers, we are merchants of morality.[91]

Goffman, like Durkheim,[92] sees mankind threatened by the possibilities of an amoral Hobbesian "war of everyman against everyman" where each is in pursuit of self-interest. He suggests, like Durkheim, the imposition of a corrective social reality of rules, regulations and "facts." For Durkheim, this was to take the form of a secular morality in the guise of the general "social order" whose values would be internalized by the individual, uniting self-interest and group-interest. Goffman also sees the existence of a coterie of social facts—except for him, they apply to the arena for the staging of performances. So we see mention of proprieties of deference and demeanor,[93] "tact" and "protective practices"[94] (the "moral" obligation to aid and accept the performance of others), and in general, a devotion to being a good actor "and not causing a scene or a disturbance" or being "*de trop* or out of place."[95] In all, these rules of interaction function in the same manner as Durkheim's social facts—that is, they are, "Types of conduct or thought which are not only external to the individual but are, moreover, endowed with coercive power, by virtue of which they impose themselves upon him..."[96] Similarly from Goffman: "Universal human nature is not a very human thing. By acquiring it, the person becomes a kind of construct, built up not from inner psychic propensities but from moral rules that are impressed upon him without."[97]

We see that while Durkheim and Goffman suggest a dual nature to man (in much the same way as Mead) they both see this duality resolved in favor of man's "social" rather than "individual" nature. Egoism and self-interest are not conducive in a Spencerian sense to social harmony. Society and the stage require adherence to collective values and rules of conduct. Interestingly, both Durkheim and Goffman see man as better off *because of* the *imposition of order*. The moral life is satisfying on all counts. It acts as a buffer against anomie and the despair that could lead one to suicide;[98] it prevents the embarrassments of actors who might be discredited and also protects audiences who witness these.[99]

We see the "ritualization" of Durkheim's *Elementary Forms* come to full fruition in Goffman's sociology. For Goffman, the "setting," the "encounter" and the "frame" all act to produce the same ceremonial sense of morality that Durkheim saw in primitive ritual. Complete with rules, traditions, habituations and generally unquestionable practices tacitly accepted by actors, the ritual of interaction represents the secularization of morality into properties of face-to-face behavior. The sense of ritual is the sense of social order; Goffman's interaction ritual is no less important in this regard than Durkheim's.

In all, Goffman is truly Durkheimian; even insofar as he reflects the same concern with "functions" that sociologists such as Parsons and Merton saw in Durkheim's work. In the most general sense, Goffman's "functionalism" is contained in his ascription of a functional imperative for effectiveness in performance. The "function" of impression is to succeed in impressing, to appear as claimed.[100] There is, in fact, a *normative* quality to performance in that it is expected that we "ought" to be as we appear to be. To be otherwise is to risk discredit and embarrassment and to violate a tacit understanding or common value we share with our audience. While several of Goffman's works generally reflect a functionalist perspective it becomes explicit in "Role Distance" when he analyzes distancing oneself from role as a functional adaptation to the exigencies of certain occupational settings.[101] Goffman maintains that commitment to the success of the situation requires role distance on our part in order to "integrate the system"[102] and meet the "claim created by the overall 'needs' of the situated activity system itself...."[103] Certainly, this is a functionalist orientation.

We have seen in this section a fairly close relationship between Durkheim's work and that of Goffman. There are, of course, notable differences.

Obviously the two sociologists are practicing vastly different sociologies. One is primarily large-scale, while the other deals in face-to-face behavior. One frequently voices a humanistic concern for the effect of societal factors on the individual, while the other is notable for his almost total lack of communication to the reader that he is genuinely interested in what happens to man. "Dramaturgy," claims Gouldner, "is not the antidote...but the symptom...."[104]

But the most important difference between these two sociologists is that while Durkheim's portrait of society is done in brush strokes of solidarity and order, Goffman suggests the impressionistic, ephemeral nature of any such solidarity and order in that it is ever in jeopardy and ever constructed anew.

PROBLEMATICS, SELF-DESTRUCTION, AND A CONSPIRACY OF EXCHANGE

When I introduced this chapter, I indicated that conventional sociological theories of social exchange were limited because of their implicit assumptions that social behavior as exchange could be seen as the unproblematic, working out of a rationality of needs or economic processes. I suggested that what was needed to make the exchange model more realistic and reflective of man's condition was focus on the uncertainty, problematics and negotiation processes experienced and enacted by real people in real situations.

Goffman provides us with this corrective. His sociology is a categorization of many of those contingencies of face-to-face behavior that make interaction and the pursuit of self-interest a gamble.

In general, the problem of interaction is the problem of situational control over the giving and giving off of impressions. "When an individual appears before others he will have many motives for trying to control the impression they receive of the situation."[105] Unfortunately, when it comes to stage craft and stage management there are precious few virtuosi. Most of us suffer from the vagaries of personal and situationally-induced incompetencies that interfere with good acting. For example: "Delivery itself is certainly a problematic and important feature, and certainly control of voice, monitoring of speech, and other physical acts are involved."[106] We also are plagued by the condition of having properly rehearsed, prepared and polished an act only to realize that our perception of reality is distorted and we have prepared to do the right act in the wrong place.[107]

Additionally, many actors suffer the effects of bringing to the interactive arena what Homans would call "bad investments": personalities that jar rather than jell, inferior rank, physical and social stigma and incapacities, and poor preparation.[108] However, in many cases, poor performances may not be "an inheritance of our animal or divine nature"[109] but "the obligatory limits definitionally associated with a particular frame."[110] The baseball umpire limited to split second frames is, thus, taxed to his performance limit,[111] as are any others who dwell in arenas where there is action—for example, con-artists, gamblers, circus performers, sexual deviates and "passers."[112]

It should be mentioned that many performances suffer relatively less from the jeopardy of dramatization. Some, like surgeons, judges, policemen and other "uniformed" services are "wonderfully adapted, from the point of view of communication, as means of vividly conveying the qualities and attributes claimed by the performer."[113] Also, many situations are so "ruled" (in both senses) by rituals of protocol and tradition that "proper execution can easily become routine and unproblematic."[114]

However, in those problematic arenas, the consequences of being discredited await those who would do a poor act.[115] Most immediately they might suffer the embarrassment and humiliation that result from this, but more crucial is the effect that "discredit" has on identity. For Goffman, there is no essential self; there is only the self that derives from the immediacy of the act and the situation.[116] Doing *is* being and it follows that a "poor show" results in some identity deprecation and self destruction.[117] Avoiding spoiled identity then would appear to be the closest thing to a human "need" in Goffman's sociology. Our interactive orientation is toward those practices that aid in this avoidance.

First among these practices is the manifestation of dramaturgical discipline, skill and competence. The capability to appear spontaneous, credible or "cool"[118] and to avoid the pitfalls of stage fright and insecurity are the marks of a seasoned actor.[119] This capability is not only protective for the performer but is also soothing to his audience. There is for example the situational discomfort experienced by those who are witness to the public ineptitude of a singer who cannot reach a note or a comic who "bombs." We "feel" good when performers are good and bad when they are bad.

Another practice employed to avoid the hazards of performance is "playing it safe." When one fears the potential for identity threat a place might hold, one is wise to avoid that place. The sensitivity for place and situation avoidance would seem to be related to the degree to which one feels that one is in some way stigmatized relative to that place.[120] Racial minorities avoid the places visited by bigots; the agnostic stays away from church, and the gang member stays off a rival gang's turf. Certainly these practices have much to do with a desire to avoid disinterest or physical abuse but a part of them is certainly responsive to an

108

attempt at identity protection. An additional way of playing it safe is to frequent only those places where enactment is so ritualized as to "write into the script" what an insecure actor would fear to improvise. Routine is often a comfort, as perhaps will attest the yet unsure teenager who seeks the womb of peer group activity, or the President's press secretary who prefers that his boss stick to the prepared speech and avoid extemporaneous opportunities for faux pas.

We also protect ourselves by such "defensive practices" as team collusion, guarding against spies and disclosure of secrets, and attempting to "rig" the show by such ploys as choosing the stage and setting up the props.[121] To the extent that we can thus impose our "directing" over that of others we have more control over the enactment.

Perhaps the most enlightening discussion of ploys intended to protect the show and, it follows, the actors' selves, is contained in what Goffman describes as "protective practices."[122] These are situations when the audience or other actors "contribute in a significant way to the maintenance of a show by exercising tact or protective practices on behalf of the performers."[123] A conspiracy exists between actors to support the source of their mutual building and maintenance of self—the situation. Often this life-game takes on light-hearted overtones as with a teacher patiently restating and oversimplifying a question that a student, misunderstanding, has just given a ludicrously inappropriate answer for. Occasionally the etiquette of discretion and tact results in actions which are "more elaborate that is the performance for which they are a response."[124] In these sorts of cases the extent to which audiences and other actors will extend themselves for the sake of the situation and its members is most apparent.

It should be noted that Goffman allows for at least three motives for extending tact to actors: (1) "identification with the performers" manifested in some display of loyalty, (2) "desire to avoid a scene" and thus violate the continuity of the show, and (3) "desire to ingratiate themselves with the performers for purposes of exploitation."[125] What is common in all cases of discretion and tactful displays and, for that matter, in all interactions not characterized by the extremes of coercion or mere reflex behavior, is the working out of a *conspiracy of exchange*. Since interaction is a gamble that is subject to all the pitfalls of performances that fail, and since each actor is typically aware of his own and others' potential for jeopardy, actors generally enter into interactions with a tacit willingness to exchange with others a tactful suspension of doubt and disbelief so that each can do his best at expressing authenticity. Not only is the self-interest of one actor thereby aided and abetted by the tact of another, but also an indebtedness is established that ordinarily ensures the second actor a degree of interactive security. So that I am not misunderstood as portraying interaction as a mere surface display of manners and etiquette, we would note that while this surface process is going on each actor is personally involved in an "information game" in which he attempts a more manipulative assessment of others' expressions, and simultaneously attempts to read others for what they "really" think of his expressions.[126] In this way, social actors are both performing and constantly assessing audience reaction to their performance. This often results in the exchange of feedback, restarts, backtracking and reentrenchments that are characteristic of many encounters. However, what may in the reality of its working out be an unsure, jerky performance exchange, typically is seen by the observer to be a smooth, orderly and normal appearance. Society may then be seen as resting comfortably on a bed of normal appearances—themselves the consequences of a much more elaborate exchange of assessments, tacit agreements and mutually self-supporting conspiracies.

SELF, PERSONALITY, FREEDOM, AND STRUCTURE: GOFFMAN'S MODEL OF MAN

The development of modern culture is characterized by the preponderance of what one may call the 'objective spirit' over the 'subjective spirit.' This is to say, in language as well as in law, in the technique of production as well as in art, in science as well as in the objects of the domestic environment, there is embodied a sum of spirit. The individual in his intellectual development follows the growth of this spirit very imperfectly and at an ever increasing distance....

The individual is reduced to a negligible quantity, perhaps less in his consciousness than in his practice and in the totality of his obscure emotional states that are derived from this practice. The individual has become a mere cog in an enormous organization of things and powers which tear from his hands all progress, spirituality, and value in order to transform them from their subjective form into the form of a purely objective life....

...life is composed more and more of these impersonal contents and offerings which tend to displace the genuine personal colorations and incomparabilities. This results in the individual's summoning the utmost in uniqueness and particularization, in order to preserve his most personal core. He has to exaggerate this personal element in order to remain audible even to himself.[127]

The kind of individualism that Simmel speaks of in this passage is indicative of elements present in Goffman's perspective on the self. In this section we will analyze how Goffman's views of self, society, freedom and structure are reflected in the two dominant lines developed through the corpus of his writings. The total picture that will emerge is, on one hand, one of the subjugation of a "possible" self (the essential, autonomous self) to the exigencies of place and situation, and, on the other hand, the frantic, desperate grasp by this situational self for its own existence.

Goffman's emphasis on the situation is intended both as a heuristic ploy that allows him to "get into" the processes of self-presentation—also as a substantive account of what he calls the "machinery of self-production."[128] This machinery is the sum of components and processes, such as region control, team collusion and audience tact—all of which contribute to the fostering of impressions about character and self. To the extent that the machinery is "well oiled...the performance will come off and the firm self accorded each performed character will appear to emanate intrinsically from its performer."[129] The actor in this process may be convinced by his own act and thus be seen as "sincere" or may be more manipulatively involved in the fostering of impressions for the sake of other ends, in which case we might consider him to be "cynical."[130] In either case, however, we note that the impressions that come to be seen as the actor's self derive from the situation and its events and not from any "essentials" of the actor himself. Goffman's view of man is not at all an existentialist one but one in which the individual as "being" is secondary to the structural qualities of the situation.[131] The only way we, as actors, can "get to" the essentials of each other's being is through the dramas of everyday life encounters—our only being is that which we present in the theater.

There are consequences to this portrayal of a prescribed self that bear on the possibilities for realizing personality and personal freedom. In dealing with the first of these, personality, we find that the term itself is seldom if ever used by Goffman. In the traditions of symbolic interactionism and dramatism he prefers to deal with the actor's "self" and "personal style."[132] Doing this, Goffman remains true to the notion of a situationally prescribed self, for, were he to deal with personality, he would tacitly concede that the individual brings to social action a starting mechanism that resides, not in action itself, but in the actor—that is, an "essential" self. While Goffman does not allow for an essential self in his dramaturgical model, he charitably concedes that the typical consequence of performing a situationally prescribed self is that the actor himself has a "feeling" for the authenticity and autonomy of what he "is." An effective actor then is not only one who is rewarded for good performances by the acceptance of his audience, but also is one who comes to see a continuity of essentials in his performances and is able to account for himself as more than a mere shell. Thus, man is ordinarily saved from the schizophrenia of realizing his unauthenticity by a Meadian believing "in himself." It is only when he can no longer sustain his own presentation *to* self that his sense of identity will suffer. This may occur on one level when the strain toward authenticity is too much to bear and the actor "breaks down," thus exposing the ephemeral nature of himself to himself.[133] The occupations of psychotherapy and counselling are often devoted to aiding the actor in rebuilding the lost sense of a real self.

What we have been describing as the subjugation of the self to the situation is the dominant theme of the self developed in Goffman's work. From the theme's earliest renditions in his doctoral dissertation, "Communication and Conduct in an Island Community," through development in early published essays (later collected in *Interaction Ritual*) to its most formalized fashion in *Presentation of Self*; and on to later works, such as *Encounters*, where it is portrayed through a repertoire of alternative roles; *Stigma, Behavior in Public Places, Strategic Interaction, Relations in Public* where the emphasis is on the techniques of impression management under various situational conditions; and, finally, in *Frame Analysis* where it takes the form of a detailed examination of the situation as a frame for organizing experience—in all these works—the primary focus on self is as a consequence of the act and the situation. The only options open to the actor who would attempt to shrug off the situation and assert something of a "real" self in this dramaturgical performance are "communications out of character," e.g., derogation of an absent actor,[134] staging talk,[135] team collusion,[136] and realigning actions[137], or totally disavowing any expressive commitment, thus thoroughly violating the situation (e.g., by intentionally "hamming it up" or just refusing to "go on stage"). Note however that each of these is less than an acceptable attempt at a "real" self; in the first (communication out of character), the actor is still bound and limited by the situation, requiring that he do some sleight-of-hand or surreptitious maneuvering to avoid, just momentarily, its hold on him; in the second case (disavowing commitment) a *sense* of self (if it at all results) is at the expense of any further *display* of self relative to that encounter—a kind of interactional cutting off of one's nose to spite one's face. While this ploy is playable by some actors some of the time, it cannot suffice as a life style for very long without destruction of the very self that is attempted.

Goffman, then, seems throughout most of his works to be specifying the impossibility of the mutual presence of an inter-actional, theatrical self and an essential self in any one actor. True, he does in the final pages of *Presentation of Self* caution the reader not to take his stage analogy "too seriously," however he very quickly notes that real stages and social situations both employ "the same techniques."

> Those who conduct face to face interaction on a theater's stage must meet the key requirement of real situations; they must expressively sustain a definition of the situation; but this they do in circumstances that have facilitated their developing an apt terminology for the interactional tasks that all of us share.[138]

Goffman, then, appears to leave the actor with "no exit" from the confines of place and situation and thus with no hope for manifesting an essential, existential self.[139]

While this last statement is seemingly an accurate portrayal of most of Goffman's work it does not apply to two writings that depart, if only slightly, from the theme we have been discussing. These are the essay, "Mental Symptoms and Public Order," and the important work, *Asylums*. In the first, Goffman explores the psychiatric labeling and treatment of psychosis, suggesting that this profession has systematically misread the essence of psychotic behavior. Rather than the defect-in-communication label that or-dinarily is pinned on this behavior, Goffman suggests that we see psychosis as a violation of "the approved patterns of manner and association or co-participation in terms of which individuals are obliged to regulate their comings together."[140] But is is not merely to point out manifestations of rule-violating behavior—such as we would see among the unmannerly, eccentric, insolent, arrogant or generally unpredictable or untrustworthy—that provide us with an understanding of psychosis, for there is "no psychotic misconduct that cannot be matched precisely in everyday life by the conduct of persons who are not psychologically ill nor considered to be so...."[141] To fully understand psychotic behavior, Goffman feels we must attend to the situation in which it occurs. Specifically, he notes:

> Mental hospitals, perhaps through a process of natural selection, are organized in such a way as to provide exactly the kind of setting in which unwilling participants have recourse to the exhibition of situational improprieties. *If you rob people of all customary means of expressing anger and alienation and put them in a place where they have never had better reason for these feelings, then the natural recourse will be to seize upon what remains—situational improprieties.* [142]

It is in this passage where Goffman comes close to an important consideration on the self that he approaches even more closely in *Asylums*; that is, that the self—the essential, existential self—exists and rears its head when it is assaulted or threatened with extinction, particularly by the demands of "total institutions."

> The practice of reserving something of oneself from the clutch of an institution is very visible in mental hospitals and prisons but can be found in more benign and less totalistic institutions, too. I want to argue that this recalcitrance is not an incidental mechanism of defense but rather *an essential constituent of the self.* [143]

While Goffman has previously depicted man as a performer with no essential self, in *Asylums, he details both the need* for such a self in all of us and the *ways* in which it is manifested. It is when the actor is faced with the full weight of degradation, mortification, discrediting and the loss of identity that he sees the need for self-survival and engages in practices such as withdrawal, intransigence, colonization and conversion—all of which are to be seen as functional adaptations to self-threatening institutional conditions, and all of which indicate the actor's need to preserve and assert the sanctity of a "real" self.[144] Self, in this context is often seen "as a stance-taking entity, a something that takes up a position somewhere between identification with an organization and opposition to it..." and thus resists in large measure the deter-

minism of place and situation.[145] "It is thus," Goffman notes in an often quoted declaration, *"against something* that the self can emerge."[146] In much the same way as Marx saw the need for "class consciousness" as a starting mechanism for the overthrow of forces of subjugation, Goffman requires that the actor recognize the jeopardy of the state he's in—his condition—before his essential self can emerge.[147]

But there is a danger of interpreting too much of a tone of Marxian resistance into Goffman's sociology. While he does describe adaptive processes, these are singularly of one character: they are attempts at *individual* and not *group* survival. Goffman's actor resists more out of fear and panic than out of a desire to overthrow or even protest. In fact, he would probably prefer to play a part that gets him "through" rather than one which places him "outside." He seeks an "underlife" of "secondary adjustments"[148] rather than organized resistance and exposure of the inequities of institutional life; he seeks to *escape* power rather than identify it and rebel.

Goffman's strengths lie in his ability at depicting the individual as interactant. When he is descriptively detailing the "work" of interaction in all its intricacies or hinting at the emergence and maintenance of self (relative to the determination of place and situation), Goffman is doing his best sociology. But there is, as earlier noted, another Goffman. This is the one who senses (particularly in *Asylums*) an element of confrontation between the individual and the structural, institutionalized aspects of society. Here Goffman is at his weakest, for he does not fully develop a sociology of structure and power of an institutional nature. Rather, the reader is left with the task of gleaning and constructing this himself out of a more particularistic analysis of a specific form of institutionalized power, the "total institution." In fairness to the author, Goffman (like Burke before him) is committed to description and not explanation, choosing to deal with structure and institutions only insofar as they provide a "frame" for action. They are important, of course, but not of immediate concern for interactional analysis. Actors are *real* in their *acts* not in the determinations of these acts. For example, Goffman (as previously noted) does not pursue Ichheiser's legacy of a sense of *why* men wear masks. Had he chosen this tack, Goffman might have been led to do more in *Asylums* than he actually accomplishes. He might, for instance, have pursued an analysis of those structural properties generically shared between total institutions and the institutions of "civil" society. As seen earlier, Urbanek (to mention one) sees a need for this in any dramaturgical analysis.

Although Goffman does not assist us much, the careful reader of *Asylums* (and "Mental Symptoms and Public Order") will be able to find the beginnings of a structural sociology—a sociology, that is, of institutions and institutional power. This beginning takes shape in each of two somewhat obscure parallel discussions: first is the occasionally stated, but more often implied similarities between the "total institutions" that Goffman describes and the other, more ordinary, institutional forms; second, is a comparison between the individual's responses to the impositions of specific total institutional power and his responses to the more generalized institutional impositions of "civil" society.

It is undeniable that *Asylums* deals with a unique form of institutional analysis. Goffman's intent is to examine those organizations whose hold on the time, space and movement of the individual is total—prisons, mental health care wards, prisoner-of-war camps, etc. Admittedly the uniqueness of settings of this type results in particularlistic forms of sociological analysis. The individual's management of identity, time and reality orientation within the walls of total institutions often requires original and unusual adaptations, all this necessitated by the unusual conditions under which he lives. However, Goffman allows us to see that his sociology occasionally attempts to generalize from these forms to more usual ones. The "avowed goals" of total institutions ("accomplishment of some economic goal; education and training; medical or psychiatric treatment; religious purification; protection of the wider community from pollution....")[149] merely reflect rational organizations consciously designed "as effective machines for producing a few...officially approved ends."[150] Furthermore, as Goffman states, "...these features are found in places other than total institutions."[151] It is not just the total institution, but, by inference and implication, *all* institutions that are characterized by such features as an imposed sequence of activities, a system of formal rulings, a body of officials and an underlying rational plan.[152] In addition, all institutions are to be seen as representing a normative orientation toward these features—i.e., there are to be found constituted notions of "right," "wrong," "good," and "bad." Indeed, Goffman maintains that "...in each total institution we can see in miniature the development of something akin to a functionalist version of moral life."[153]

In the end, Goffman fails at extending this incipient structural sociology to the point where it might stand by itself as the needed corrective to the particularism of interactional analysis. True, the author does transmit the direction he might have taken with such claims as, "...a total institution functions somewhat as a state...,"[154] and "...every institution has encompassing tendencies,"[155] yet he appears to falter at doing the kind of *critical, analytical* sociology that would realize the potential of such implications.

While Goffman's primary failing may be said to be his lack of commitment to a fully developed structural sociology, he does give attention to the individual adaptations by actors that such a sociology would perhaps imply. Part of *Asylums* deals perceptively with aspects of the inmate's solution to the problems of survival and personal effectiveness under the yoke of institutional power.

Goffman's general position is that actors in total institutions behave so as to default from "prescribed being";[156] that is, they engage in "secondary adjustments"[157] and an "underlife"[158] of non-prescribed behavior that allows them elbow room in their day-to-day oppressions.

We find that participants decline in some way to accept the official view of what they should be putting into and getting out of the organization and, behind this, of what sort of self and world they are to accept for themselves. Where enthusiasm is expected, there will be apathy; where loyalty, there will be disaffection; where attendance, absenteeism; where robustness, some kind of illness;

where deeds are to be done, varieties of inactivity. We find a multitude of homely little histories, each in its way a movement of liberty. Whenever worlds are laid on, underlives develop.[159]

That these modes of behavior characterize human adaptation to institutional requisites surely depict a *general* need responsive to a *general* condition. Indeed, Goffman notes that, "These adjustments can and do arise in connection with the individual's bondage to other types of social entity,"[160] for example, the state, marriage, and legality. In fact, as we have already noted, it is Goffman's contention that it is only when the individual comes up *against* something that his essential self can emerge.[161] Yet, here, Goffman has again returned his analysis to the safer confines of "total" institutions. His comments on the adaptive processes and an emergent self are primarily restricted to arenas where the fight is pointed, blatant and undeniable. Goffman, again, fails at extending his reach beyond specific settings and into a world of diffuse, covert, and everyday examples of adaptation to institutional power. Instead he leaves us with the tantalizing, unanswered question, "May this not be the situation....in free society, too?"[162]

It is ironic that a theorist who is capable of infinite and detailed perception of the intricacies and nuances of interaction and who has sporadically in his works done more than hint at broader applicability of microsocial analysis, cannot see, or does not wish to see, the implications of total institution analysis when applied to more general structural and institutional issues.[163] On the contrary, Goffman constantly reminds us of the differences between the inmate world and "civil" society. For example; "In civil society, an individual pushed to the wall in one of his social roles usually has an opportunity to crawl into some protected place where he can indulge in commercialized fantasy...or employ 'relievers'...." Surely, Goffman would not characterize recent activist protestations by various oppressed groups "pushed to the wall" as the search for "fantasy" or "relievers."

Goffman himself suggests the direction and contribution that his unique, valuable form of interactive description and analysis *might* pursue when he points out that, "Inmates must be caused to *self-direct* themselves in a manageable way, and for this to be promoted, both desired and undesired conduct must be defined as springing from the personal will and character of the individual inmate himself...."[164] Here, Goffman is portraying more than just total institutions. He is unmistakingly identifying the general dynamic of socialization and internalization to be found among all of society's institutionalized representations. It is to an analysis of the effectiveness of these structures and their programs of employing institutional power that Goffman might fruitfully apply his skills.

CONCLUSION

We are left then with the question of where Goffman stands on all this. Is he the functionalist who attends to the structures and functions of situations and their men? Is he the naturalist who ethnographs humans? Is he the drama critic who frames all of social life as a stage analogy? Is he the humanist who shows a concern for man's condition in the world? Or is he a cop out who shirks the tension between the individual and his society by reducing each of them to elements of the situation and by making this situation devoid of any value other than appearance and effective performance?[165] I remark about the complexity of Goffman's sociology to observe that in many ways he is each of these.

I have presented Goffman's dramaturgy as a needed corrective for deficiencies previously identified in the writings of the two major theorists of the exchange processes of human behavior. The theories of both Homans and Blau were seen to contain epistemological and methodological deficiencies and limitations that made the exchange model an unrealistic and tenuous attempt at a comprehensive identification and analysis of basic social processes. Specifically, both of these theorists emphasize, often to exclusivity, the exigencies of schemata containing unproblematic portraits of the dynamics of human behavior. From these perspectives, interaction was depicted as the working out of one form or another of a rationality of needs (seen either as biologically or psychologically determinative) or a rationality of economic motives and processes.

I have suggested that such portraits as Homans and Blau present lack a sense of, and allowance for, the realistic, "processual" and often non-rational properties of human behavior. Such properties are subsumed under the concepts of uncertainty, problematics and negotiation, and are behaviorally reflected by such manifestations as pursuit, attempt and mutually supportive exchanges.

While Homans and Blau emphasize determinants and motivations, Goffman is seen to offer the student of human behavior a model by which to describe and, to some extent, interpret the dynamics of the processes in which these and other motives are enacted. Such a model, if it is to be at all reflective of real-life exigencies and real-life processes, should result in a detailed picture of day-to-day, face-to-face activity insofar as that activity characterizes what actors actually do vis à vis other actors. Such a model should also be sensitive to the nuances and intricacies of the point and counterpoint of everyday exchanges, negotiations, balances and imbalances. In the accomplishment of these tasks, Goffman shows a rare observational genius—one which has inspired emulation from both advocates and detractors.

But there should be another part to such a model. This is the confrontation between the individual actor and the structural and institutional demands and limitations on his enactments that his society thrusts upon him. Here Goffman has not been as successful. For, while he has appealingly and pointedly described this individual versus structure contest as it appears in arenas of extremes, he has hesitated to develop a structural sociology that would enable explicit generalization to the more ordinary and subtle structures and institutions of civil society. As a sociologist of the drama of everyday activity, Goffman's concern for structure is self-limiting in the confines of the stage. Once having identified structures and institutions as "frames" for activity, Goffman then attends almost exclusively to that activity and leaves it for others to investigate the institutional properties of stages.

In the end, Goffman has contributed a needed corrective to an attempt at seeing the exchange processes of human behavior. He has clearly (and most appealingly) portrayed the problematic aspects of interaction and of the preservation of a sense of self in that interaction. In doing this he has paid attention to the fact that in most interactive contexts and usually in spite of the potential for mutually exclusive pursuits of self-interest, men tend to conspire to exchange with each other such forgivings and supports as are necessary to maintain the sanctity and continuity of the situation. For it is in such continuity that all men derive a sense of well-being and even a sense of identity. Whatever be their individual wanderings and maneuverings within situational confines, actors typically cooperate to support these confines. It is only when the situation becomes maximally oppressive and self-threatening that they will seek relief in an underlife that allows them the leeway to "make it" in each of two worlds—one, the institutional, prescribed world that they cannot physically escape and the other, the periodic departures into secret places.

For present purposes we should note a final, yet important limitation of Goffman's work, that bears on the development of our more general concerns in this work: that is the culture-bound quality of Goffman's dramaturgy. Impression management and self-presentation may aptly describe the cultural ways of the modern urban Western world, but they surely are not adequate for all cultures and all times. What we are now looking for is a sociology that will complete the generic exchange model by accounting for invariant features of human social behavior such that a final statement of universal application can be attempted. We will seek such a perspective in the ethnomethodology of Harold Garfinkel.

NOTES

1. Erving Goffman, *The Presentation of Self in Everyday Life*, (Garden City, New York: Doubleday Anchor Books, 1959). An earlier version of this book was first published as a monograph at the Social Sciences Research Center at the University of Edinburgh in 1956.
2. See "On Cooling the Mark Out," *Psychiatry* 15 (1952), pp. 451–63; "Communication and Conduct in an Island Community," unpublished doctoral dissertation, Department of Sociology, The University of Chicago, 1953; "On Face Work: An Analysis of Ritual Elements in Social Interaction" and "Embarassment and Social Organization," *American Journal of Sociology* 62 (1956), pp. 264–71; "The Nature of Deference and Demeanor," *American Anthropologist* 58 (June 1956), pp. 473–502; "Alienation from Interaction," *Human Relations* 10 (1957), pp. 47–60; *Encounters* (Indianapolis, Ind.: The Bobbs-Merrill Co., Inc., 1961); *Behavior in Public Places* (New York: The Free Press, 1963); *Stigma: Notes on the Management of Spoiled Identity* (Englewood Cliffs, New Jersey: Prentice-Hall, 1963); *Interaction Ritual* (Chicago: Aldine, 1967); *Strategic Interaction* (New York: Ballantine Books, 1969); *Relations in Public (New York: Harper & Row, 1972); Frame Analysis: An Essay on the Organization of Experience* (Cambridge, Mass.: Harvard University Press, 1974).
3. One, however, notes a deterioration of style from earlier lucid efforts to the more obscure and stylistically deficient *Frame Analysis*.
4. *Asylums* (Garden City, New York: Doubleday Anchor Books, 1961). "Mental Symptoms and Public Order," in *Interaction Ritual*, originally published in *Disorders of Communication* (Research Publications, Association for Research in Nervous and Mental Disease) 42 (1964), pp. 262–69.
5. Goffman, *Presentation of Self*, p. 25.
6. Ibid., p. 56.
7. Ibid., p. 216.
8. Specifically developed in *Presentation of Self*.
9. Primarily from Kenneth Burke, *A Grammar of Motives* (Englewood Cliffs, N.J.: Prentice-Hall, 1945). See also the author's *Permanence and Change* (Indianapolis: Bobbs-Merrill, 1935, 1965), and *A Rhetoric of Motives* (Englewood Cliffs, N.J.: Prentice-Hall, 1950).
10. Gustav Ichheiser, "Misunderstandings in Human Relations: A Study in False Social Relations," supplement to *The American Journal of Sociology* 55 (September, 1949).
11. Ibid., p. 64.
12. Ibid., p. 7.
13. Ichheiser, p. 67.
14. See for example, John O'Neill, "Self-Prescription and Social Machiavellianism" in his *Sociology as a Skin Trade* (New York: Harper and Row, 1972), pp. 11–19. See also, Peter L. Berger and Thomas Luckmann.

The Social Construction of Reality pp. 205–206, n. 15 in which the authors argue that Goffman's "role distance" is only possible from elements learned through secondary socialization (the internalization of "institution-based subworlds"), and is not possible from those aspects of one's "self" which are derived through primary socialization.

15. Edward Urbanek, "Roles, Masks and Characters: A Contribution to Marx's Idea of the Social Role," in Peter L. Berger, ed., *Marxism and Sociology: Views From Eastern Europe* (New York: Appleton-Century-Crofts, 1969), pp. 168–201.
16. Ibid., p. 176.
17. Ibid., p. 172.
18. See especially Burke, *A Grammar of Motives*.
19. Burke specifies that his dramatism is to be seen both as a technique for getting at what is going on *and* as an ontological depiction of the human condition. See for example his comments in "Dramatism" in *The Encyclopedia of the Social Sciences*, 1968, pp. 445–451.
    Stanford M. Lyman and Marvin B. Scott make this point in *The Drama of Social Reality* (New York: Oxford Univ. Press, 1975), p. 168 n. 1.
20. Burke, *Permanence and Change*, p. 35.
21. Peter L. Berger, *Invitation to Sociology* (Garden City, New York: Doubleday Anchor, 1963), p. 96.
22. Ibid., p. 98.
23. Burke, *Permanence and Change*, p. 29, (my emphasis). For an illuminating elaboration of this perspective on motive see the discussion of "accounts" by Lyman and Scott in *A Sociology of the Absurd* (New York: Appleton-Century-Crofts, 1970), pp. 11–144.
24. Burke, *A Grammar of Motives*, pp. XVII–XXV.
25. See Goffman, *Frame Analysis*.
26. Burke, *Permanence and Change*, p. 162 (my emphasis).
27. Burke, *A Grammar of Motives*, p. X (my emphasis).
28. Goffman, *Presentation of Self*, p. 244.
29. Ibid., p. 245.
30. Lyman and Scott (*The Drama of Social Reality*) note that Goffman's use of dramaturgy is only as metaphor and not as ontology which "excludes the theoretical generality inherent in dramatism." (p. 169, n. 2). Lyman elsewhere suggests that a proper "frame" for Goffman's dramaturgy is "civilization," certainly an extension of the frame Goffman adopts. (See Stanford M. Lyman, "Civilization: Contents, Discontents, Malcontents," review essay in *Contemporary Sociology* 2 (July 1973), pp. 360–366).
    Goffman would appear to have responded to Lyman's suggestion in his recent *Frame Analysis* (p. 8) when he states "any event can be described in terms of a focus that includes a wide swath or a narrow one...And no one has a theory as to what particular span and level will come to be the ones employed. To begin with, I must be allowed to pick my span and level arbitrarily, without special justification."
31. Goffman notes the inadequacies of the "Stage Model" in his "Preface" to *Presentation of Self*. "The stage presents things that are make-believe; presumably life presents things that are real...."
32. Goffman, *Presentation of Self*, p. 243.

33. Ibid., p. 251.
34. Specifically, in George Herbert Mead, *Mind, Self, and Society* (Chicago: The University of Chicago Press, 1934). Also see Mead's *The Philosophy of the Present* (La Salle, Ill.: Open Court Publishing Co.,1932), and *The Philosophy of the Act* (Chicago: The University of Chicago Press, 1938).
35. Mead, *Mind, Self, and Society*, p. 49.
36. Ibid., p. 50.
37. Ibid., p. 226.
38. Ibid., p. 210.
39. Ibid., p. 210.
40. See "Supplementary Essay II," ibid., pp. 347–353.
41. Here I obviously disagree with Wrong's assessment of Mead's work as an emphasis on man the acceptance-seeker who is *thoroughly* responsive to the impressions others have of him. See Dennis Wrong, "The Oversocialized Conception of Man in Modern Sociology."
42. See, Mead, *Mind, Self, and Society*, p. 210.
43. Goffman, *Presentation of Self*, p. 56.
44. Ibid., p. 57.
45. Ibid., p. 168.
46. Ibid., p. 210.
47. Ibid., p. 216.
48. Ibid., p. 216.
49. Ibid., p. 217.
50. Goffman, "Role Distance," in *Encounters*.
51. Ibid., p. 142.
52. Ibid., p. 143.
53. Goffman, "The Neglected Situation" in J. Gumperz and D. Hymes, eds. *The Ethnography of Communication, American Anthropologist* 66[6] part 2 (1964), p. 134, (as quoted in Peter K. Manning, review essay of *Relations in Public, The Sociological Quarterly* 14 (Winter 1973), pp. 135–143.
54. Goffman, *Frame Analysis*, pp. 573–574 (my emphasis).
55. Ibid., pp. 1–2.
56. Ibid., p. 13.
57. Goffman, *Interaction Ritual*, p. 3.
58. See, for example, Durkheim, *Suicide*, trans. J.A. Spaulding and G. Simpson (New York: The Free Press of Glencoe, 1951), in which Durkheim stipulates a social policy intent (see especially, Book 3, Chapter 3). Also, consider his more general concerns with the erosion of social stability and anomie.
59. Robert A. Nisbet, *The Sociology of Emile Durkheim* (New York: Oxford University Press, 1974), p. 14.
60. See Emile Durkheim, *The Rules of Sociological Method* (New York: The Free Press, 1966), p. 20.
61. Durkheim, *The Elementary Forms of the Religious Life*, p. 29.
62. Durkheim, *Suicide*, p. 213.
63. Durkheim, *Rules*, p. 103.
64. Ibid., Chapters I and II; Durkheim, *Suicide*, pp. 313–315.
65. Durkheim, *Rules*, p. 14.
66. Durkheim, *Suicide*, p. 313.
67. Durkheim, *Rules*, p. lvi (emphasis mine).

68. Ibid., p. xliii, (emphasis mine).
69. Ibid., p. xlv (emphasis mine).
70. Durkheim, *The Division of Labor*, p. 399.
71. Ibid., p. 228.
72. A theme extended empirically in Durkheim, *Suicide*.
73. See Durkheim, *Division of Labor*, "Conclusion," especially pp. 472–473.
74. Emile Durkheim, *Education and Sociology* (New York: The Free Press, 1956), p. 89.
75. Durkheim, *Division of Labor*, pp. 42–43.
76. Ibid., p. 3.
77. Ibid., p. 4.
78. Durkheim, *Suicide*, p. 255.
79. Durkheim, *Elementary Forms*, p. 237 (see also the author's *Division of Labor*, p. 130, and *Suicide*, p. 319).
80. Durkheim's corrective for the deleterious consequences of modern individualism is the "corporation" or, professional association that would re-establish the bond between the individual and the social order. (See the preface to the second edition of *Division of Labor*).

    For a recent debate on the issues of individualism and freedom in Durkheim's writings, see: Whitney Pope, "Classic on Classic: Parsons' Interpretation of Durkheim," *American Sociological Review* 38 (1973), pp. 399–415. (Pope claims that Parsons' portrayal of voluntarism in Durkheim's writings is, at best, overstated); also, Jere Cohen, "Moral Freedom through Understanding in Durkheim," *American Sociological Review* 40 (1975), pp. 104–106. (Cohen sees freedom in Durkheim as deriving from the coupling of a moral base with science); also, Talcott Parsons, "Comment on Pope and Cohen," *American Sociological Review* 40 (1975), pp. 106–111.
81. This term is used here in the sense in which it is developed in Mead's, *Mind, Self and Society*.
82. Durkheim, *Elementary Forms*, p. 239.
83. See, for example, Durkheim, *Rules*, p. 2., "of course when I fully consent and conform to them [social facts], this constraint is felt only slightly, if at all, and is therefore unnecessary."
84. Durkheim, *Elementary Forms*, p. 239.
85. Durkheim, *Division of Labor*, p. 75.
86. Ibid., pp. 77–78.
87. Durkheim, *Rules*, pp. lvi–lvii, n. 7 (emphasis added).
88. Durkheim, *Division of Labor*, p. 80.
89. Mead, *Mind, Self and Society*, pp. 77–80.
90. Primarily in Durkheim, *Elementary Forms*. See also the author's *Rules*.
91. Goffman, *Presentation of Self*, p. 162.
92. See, Durkheim, *Division of Labor*, pp. 203–204.
93. Goffman, "The Nature of Deference and Demeanor."
94. Goffman, *Presentation of Self*, pp. 13–14, and *in passim*.
95. Goffman, *Behavior in Public Places*, p. 11.
96. Durkheim, *Rules*, pp. 1–3.
97. Goffman, "On Face Work," in *Interaction Ritual*, p. 45.
98. See Durkheim, *Suicide*.
99. Goffman, *Presentation of Self*, pp. 13–14.

100. Ibid., p. 6.
101. "Role Distance" in *Encounters*, pp. 120–121. Here, for example, Goffman discusses the "functions" of role distance in the surgical theater.
102. Ibid., p. 121.
103. Ibid., p. 121.
104. Alvin W. Gouldner, *The Coming Crisis of Western Sociology* (New York: Avon Books, 1970), p. 384.
105. Goffman, *Presentation of Self*, p. 15.
106. Goffman, *Frame Analysis*, p. 569.
107. Jarvie writes of members of Melanasian cargo cults who suffer from the effects of perceiving a "logic of the situation" based on input (e.g., knowledge and beliefs) which is false, and thus fruitlessly await the return of planes to airstrips they have carved out of the jungle. See I.C. Jarvie, *The Revolution in Anthropology* (London: Routledge & Kegan Paul, 1964).
108. See Goffman, *Stigma*.
109. Goffman, *Frame Analysis*, p. 573.
110. Ibid., p. 573.
111. Goffman *Presentation of Self*, p. 30.
112. Goffman, "Where The Action Is."
113. Goffman, *Presentation of Self*, p. 31.
114. Goffman, *Frame Analysis*, p. 568.
115. Goffman, *Presentation of Self*, p. 156.
116. We will deal with this topic in the next section of this chapter.
117. Goffman is obviously reflecting the Meadian tradition of self as a social product which is built up from a history of reactions to us by others. It follows, then, that poor reactions are capable of tearing down what good reactions have built up. "Ordinary body movements are seen as a direct symptom, expression, or instance of the doer's being..." (Goffman, *Frame Analysis*, p. 569).
118. See "Coolness in Everyday Life" in Lyman and Scott, *A Sociology of the Absurd*, pp. 145–158.
119. See "Stage Fright and the Problem of Identity" in ibid., pp. 145–158.
120. An interesting perspective on the degree to which such situational sensitivity can aid performers is implied in Thorstein Veblen's essay, "The Intellectual Pre-Eminence of Jews in Modern Europe," *Political Science Quarterly* (March 1919), reprinted in Leon Ardzrooni, ed. *Our Changing Order* (New York: Viking Press, 1934). Here Veblen argues that the Jew, suffering from a loss of security "in the scheme of conventions into which he has been born," develops the objectivity that often comes with marginality and becomes "a disturber of the intellectual peace."
121. Goffman, *Presentation of Self*, pp. 212–228.
122. Ibid., pp. 229–237.
123. Ibid., p. 234.
124. Ibid., p. 233.
125. Ibid., p. 232.
126. See Goffman, *Strategic Interaction*.
127. Georg Simmel, "The Metropolis and Mental Life," in *The Sociology of Georg Simmel*, p. 422.

128. Goffman, *Presentation of Self*, p. 253.
129. Ibid.
130. Ibid., pp. 17–21.
131. This point is also made by Peter K. Manning in his essay, "Existential Sociology," *The Sociological Quarterly* 14 (Spring 1973), pp. 200–225.
132. Goffman, *Role Distance*, p. 152.
133. Interestingly, Lyman and Scott (*The Drama of Social Reality*, p. 110) suggest that when actors "experience a suspension in their own belief in the naturalism or 'authenticity' of a performance put on by themselves [e.g., stage fright] or others [e.g., by unmasking] they approach a phenomenological understanding of the dramatic fundament of human existence." One implication of this is that those persons who, by reason of the constancy of dramaturgic jeopardy such as physical or social stigma, are frequently marginal to the show may have a greater "sensitivity" to this dramatic fundament. Related to this is the argument previously noted of Veblen in "The Intellectual Pre-eminence of Jews in Modern Europe."
134. Goffman, *Presentation of Self*, pp. 170–175.
135. Ibid., pp. 175–176.
136. Ibid., pp. 176–190.
137. Ibid., pp. 190–206.
138. Ibid., p. 255.
139. See Jean Paul Sartre's "No Exit," the English version by Stuart Gilbert (New York: Knopf, 1946) pp. 3–61.
140. Goffman, "Mental Symptoms and Public Order," in *Interaction Ritual*, p. 143.
141. Ibid., p. 147.
142. Ibid., p. 147 (emphasis added).
143. Goffman, *Asylums*, p. 319.
144. Ibid., pp. 61–64.
145. Ibid., p. 320.
146. Ibid., p. 320 (emphasis original).
147. Goffman seems to feel that many of us need a periodic renewal of jeopardy even when institutions are not seen as providing it. We seek places "where the action is" so that we can, as it were, test the mettle of ourselves, (in this regard see Lyman and Scott, "Adventures," in *The Drama of Social Reality*, Chapter 8, pp. 147–58).

    A related, but somewhat different form of self-seeking is what Goffman calls "away" (*Behavior in Public Places*, pp. 69–75). Here the individual withdraws from the "real or serious world" into "a playlike world in which he alone participates." Thus, he effectively escapes for the moment "all public concrete matters within the situation" by going away into a world of self.
148. Goffman, *Asylums*, p. 189.
149. Ibid., p. 83.
150. Ibid., p. 74.
151. Ibid., p. 6.
152. Ibid., p. 6.
153. Ibid., p. 87.
154. Ibid., p. 77.

155. Ibid., p. 4.
156. Ibid., p. 188.
157. Ibid., p. 189.
158. Ibid., p. 199.
159. Ibid., p. 304–305.
160. Ibid., p. 197.
161. Ibid., p. 320.
162. Ibid., p. 320.
163. See particularly Goffman's concluding comments on viewing "all of social life" from the perspective he develops in his paper, "On Cooling the Mark Out."
164. Goffman, *Asylums*, p. 87.
165. Young argues that Goffman's detachment allows him to uncover the ills that others might then see fit to criticize. [See T.R. Young, "The Politics of Sociology: Gouldner, Goffman and Garfinkel," in Denissof, Callahan, and Levine, eds., *Theories and Paradigms in Contemporary Sociology* (Itasca, Illinois: Peacock, 1974), pp. 431–41].

F I V E : : *An Exchange of Communication : Permanence and Change in the Ethnomethodology of Harold Garfinkel*

INTRODUCTION

In the last chapter, I discussed the work of Erving Goffman as it offers a corrective for deficiencies or weaknesses in an attempt at seeing social behavior as exchange processes. Specifically, Goffman's dramaturgy was seen to depict the drama of interaction as replete with problematics and the actor as ever attempting to manage those aspects of his performance whose perfection was never guaranteed but whose jeopardy was inherent in the attempt. The exigencies of such a condition are seen to give rise to exchange processes entailing the mutuality of appearance and support. Actors, mutually recognizing their shared precariousness, conspire to augment and support the enactments and identities of their fellows. By attending to "whatever can go wrong," Goffman adds the needed corrective to those models of exchange behavior premised upon the more or less unproblematic working out of assumed rationalities of need or economics.

I suggested that for whatever contributions Goffman's work

130

makes in this one direction, it is yet inadequate for completing the picture. Goffman's sociology suffers a boundedness that derives from the very strengths of its attempts. Paramount in the dramatic analogy is an abiding emphasis on the situation, the context, and in Goffman's case, the culture. While this dependence works to advantage in that it enables the theorist to get to the effects of context on behavior, it does so to the exclusion of concerns that might offer a broader, perhaps even a universal portrayal of social behavior. Situations, contexts and cultures are not the same and it is not sufficient to merely say that interaction "follows" them; if this were the only factor in the determination of forms of human behavior we would expect different forms for each different situation and the same forms under the same kinds of situation. While it is certainly not defensible to maintain that men all are the same, once we control for variations in culture and stage of societal development what ever differences appear in the actual forms of behavior would appear to be more of degree than kind. The aborigine who out of some combination of awe, fear, routine and tradition pays homage to some "pagan" representation of a "great plan" is ontologically not so very different from his more "sophisticated" churchgoing counterpart, or even the practitioner of the most complex pursuit of knowledge for whom scientism is the new god. Likewise, in the relations of one man to another the self-same processes of the intersubjective sharing of a meaning of "what is going on" take place. While Newfoundland outport fishermen may have little in common culturally with highpowered Madison Avenue advertising executives, the need of making known to their others their respective fears of drowning or suffering a metaphorical drowning in a sudden wave of budgetary cutbacks makes it necessary for each to enter into processes of exchanging communication intersubjectively meaningful among their cohorts. (These examples are drawn from the author's personal observations.)

What we seek then is a perspective on the *invariant* aspects of interaction so that these aspects might lend an air of universality to our portrayal of exchange processes. Since contexts, situations and cultures vary, we must attend to aspects *within* the frame of interaction itself, treating these aspects as phenomena for study and seeking such analyses, explanations and portrayals as support for a view of interaction that consists of invariant processes. Following this orientation, the present chapter examines the ethnomethodological studies of Harold Garfinkel to find out what contributions his approach makes to the study of invariance.

The organization of this chapter is as follows: first, we will trace Garfinkel's work back to its sources, disclosing an interesting interweaving of seemingly divergent perspectives (these dependencies will be elaborated so that the connectedness between them and Garfinkel's unique perspective will come clear); second, we will attempt to support a view of Garfinkel's work as representative of a transituational, context-free portrayal of invariant features of interaction; and, finally, we will interpret Garfinkel's ethnomethodology as it represents an *exchange of communication*—such communication built upon the very invariant processes previously identified and explicted.

It is perhaps necessary to indicate what will not be attempted in this chapter. First of all, we will be dealing with Garfinkel's ethnomethodology—*not ethnomethodology in general.* In many ways the development within this paradigm[1] has taken many different directions since Garfinkel's formative work, going from Sacks' interest in linguistic structures,[2] to Zimmerman and Pollner's emphasis on members' practices,[3] to the Blum and McHugh investigations of theory as displays of mind,[4] and on to Cicourel's depiction of basic cognitive structures and procedures.[5] To attempt an analysis of all these and other forms of ethnomethodology would be an extensive undertaking and is unnecessary. My intent is not to detail the many directions the paradigm has spawned but to examine its general contributions to the concerns of this work. I believe this is obtainable through an examination of the first and, conceptually, the most general reach among ethnomethodological works—those of Harold Garfinkel.

Another caveat is necessary: ethnomethodology, by virtue of its appeal as a revolutionary alternative to conventional sociology,

132

has elicited countless and often misleading reactionary responses from conventional sociologists. These, in turn, have on occasion enjoined ethnomethodologists to respond either supportive of or in denial of their work as being seen as an essential critique.[6] There is no particular interest here to enter into the fray by taking sides in this issue; however, to understand fully the emergence of the ethnomethodological paradigm, we will, like Kuhn,[7] see a new paradigm, in part, as a reaction to or alternative to what has come before. We begin, then, with an examination of sources and elaborations.

SOURCES AND ELABORATIONS

The Ethnomethodological Critique

> ... we do not set out from what men say, imagine, conceive, nor from men as narrated, thought of, imagined, conceived, in order to arrive at men in the flesh. We set out from real, active men.[8]

Garfinkel's ethnomethodology, procedurally (if not theoretically) first outlined in *Studies in Ethnomethodology*, is a phenomenological approach to knowing, an investigation by means ordinary and strange of methods by which functioning members make sense of their world and come to share this sense with other members.[9] Its methods are essentially empirically derived demonstrations, experiments and accounts that seek to disclose: (1) the nature of and extent to which various orders of meanings are *carried* in ordinary and common everyday exchanges of utterances,[10] (2) the *underlying sense of meaning* tacitly accepted yet ordinarily unacknowledged by members involved in communication, (3) the *exchange* of intersubjectively meaningful *understanding* derived from communication, and (4) the nature of everyday exchanges as they constitute for members a sense of a *rational, rule-like character* and thus are seen by members as making "sense." The manufacturing of, the sharing of and the tacit acceptance of meaning carried in conversation is seen as the determinant of social action. Garfinkels' work is essentially a cognitive model of how perception is organized in ways that typically result in meaningful action.

By attending to features of ordinary exchanges of communication as evidence for underlying and basic meaning-endowing processes, by treating such exchanges as phenomena distinct from their contexts, and by deliberately and assiduously avoiding the determinants on behavior of such "external" elements as power, authority and biography, Garfinkel has narrowed the concerns of those who would observe man's social behavior solely to the perceptual and cognitive processes of meaning-endowing.[11] Yet, this is not all. Seeing appearances, such as communication and interaction processes, as transituational and context-free leads Garfinkel to search for "the atemporal, *invariant forms* that run throughout the manifested appearances of things."[12] If Garfinkel is successful in this search, he will have contributed that sense of invariance and universality that we presently seek as an essential element in a framework of social behavior as exchange.

Garfinkel's program places him and his ethnomethodology in direct confrontation with other forms of sociology. As a study of "practical reasoning," ethnomethodology proposes the mutuality of the "process" of communicating meaning and the "products" of such communication.[13] In effect, then, ethnomethodology is in direct opposition to those approaches that view society and its elements as sui generis, claiming instead that there is no reality and externality to society-as-product, rather, that members come to *believe* and *accept* the existence of such reality through the very processes by which they communicate with other members. The objectivity of the world is thus seen as an accomplishment, the result of "work," or "doing" by which members account for and describe a reality, and as such has no existence independent of such accounting and describing practices. Social structure, norms, authority, power—all those traditional concerns of sociology—are recast as the consequences of interpretive procedures used by members to sustain a sense of reality. Thus, Garfinkel is not concerned with social structure or order as such, but with a search for the procedural rules that permit members to exchange communication with each other *as if* there were structure and order.

This program places ethnomethodology in a position of challenging most of the history of how sociology has been done. For sociologists are to be seen as possessing no abilities different from those of other "practical theorists." A sociologist is seen as imparting a distinctively arbitrary reification of those aspects of society he sets out to study. Sociologists are those who construct for *their* distinct meaning-endowing practices certain methodological and epistemological biases intended to disclose realities so far "hidden" in an objectified social world. Doing the "work" of sociology is, for Garfinkel, to create and sustain a *sense* of such an objectified world; and sociology's version of this world is not to be taken as *the* one, but only one of many. As he wrote in 1952: "The question is not one of what is the objective world and what is objective knowledge but what are the varieties of objective worlds and what are the varieties of objective knowledge.[14] For Garfinkel, doing sociology's version of the objective world is merely to demonstrate "mastery of natural language" (i.e., particulars of members' talk and conduct specific to practical situations) and may in no way be seen as any more than this.[15] Garfinkel terms such attempts as "constructive analyses,"[16] suggesting that they are "practical achievements through and through"[17] and, as such, tell us more about sociology and the sociologist than they do about any possible world of things. Constructive analytical accounts aim at portraying, according to Garfinkel:

> what the members' actions will have come to by using the stable structures—i.e., what they *came* to—as a point of theoretical departure from which to portray the necessary character of the pathways whereby the end result is assembled. Hierarchies of need dispositions and common culture as enforced rules of action, are favored devices for bringing the problem of necessary inference to terms, although at the cost of making out the person-in-society to be a judgmental dope.[18]

135

An essential irony to be seen in the work of conventional sociology is that as a science methodologically and epistemologically geared to distinguishing between objective expressions that hold true in a "real" world and "indexical expressions"[19] (i.e., accounts whose meaning is inseparable from the occasions of their use and are thus reflexively linked to the meaning carried in such occasions) sociology unavoidably and irremediably substitutes for members' indexicals its own.[20] Thus, devoted to the repair of indexical expressions for the purpose of getting away from the variability of members' subjective accounts and on to objective "facts," sociologists become members themselves by creating and sustaining a sense of the objectivity they seek. Ethnomethodology, by treating *all* accounts (including those of the sociologist) as part of natural languages and thus phenomenalizing communication trans-situationally, presents itself as an "alternative to . . . the central task of general theory building in professional sociology.[21]

Some caution is appropriate. Ethnomethodology has occasionally been misrepresented as (1) a "check" on scientific methodology in terms of assessing the reliability and validity of supposedly bias-free techniques, (2) a recommendation of techniques that are less obtrusive as a remedy for the problems potential in (1), and (3) an approach analogous to traditional forms of interactionist sociologies.[22] It is none of these; and, furthermore, is in Marxian terminology a "scandal and abomination"[23] to conventional sociologies,

> because it includes in its comprehension an affirmative recognition of the existing state of things, at the same time also, the recognition of the negation of that state, of its inevitable breaking up; because it regards every historically developed social form as in fluid movement, and therefore takes into account its transient nature not less than its momentary existence; because it lets nothing impose upon it, and is in essence critical and revolutionary.[24]

As a "critical and revolutionary" approach among attempts at understanding the nature of social behavior Garfinkel's ethnomethodology contains some interesting analogies to Marxist philosophy. While their practical interests are obviously quite different, Marx and Garfinkel share many of the same orientations in respect to the sociology of knowledge in their works. For each, the essential premise on which their approaches are based is the recognition that social being is determinant of social consciousness. For Marx this takes the form of taking-for-granted and reifying false consciousnesses into "ideologies," while for Garfinkel knowledge and meaning are seen to derive from the contexts in which they are produced and sustained—with no existence outside of these sustaining contexts. To both theorists knowledge and meaning are not accountable in terms of "real" properties of an objectified world, but rather in terms of the processes of communication by which this knowledge and meaning are produced. Such production involves real men in real situations intersubjectively sharing the results of negotiated processes of deciding what-the-world-is-really-like. With both Marx and Garfinkel, there is no knowledge and no meaning that is disinterested. All forms of knowing are inextricably linked to their sources, be they bourgeois ideologies of capitalism or rules of decisions used by jurors.[25] And to realize this is to realize the impossibility of getting to "literal descriptions"[26] without "breaching"[27] the existent taken-for-granted reality. Marx proposes to do this breaching conceptually by means of the *dialectic* that confronts things-as-they-are, making them problematic, and by *praxis* that asserts as action or revolutionary policy an informed awareness of the "real" world. Garfinkel suggests that those who would attend to the background expectancies of commonplace scenes might heed Schutz' admonition and become a "stranger" to "life as usual" through such means as making "trouble," producing "bewilderment," "consternation," "confusion" and generally causing interaction to become "disorganized."[28] This, he says, "should tell us something about how the structures of everyday activities are ordinarily and routinely produced and maintained."[29] For Garfinkel, breaching the rules not only challenges them but also discloses the out-of-rule behaviors (Garfinkel refers to some of these as "et cetera," "unless" and "let it pass") that members ordinarily employ in efforts to sustain the adequacy of their descriptions of what-is-going-on.[30]

While I do not wish to strain this analogy between Marx and Garfinkel by applying too much of my "reconstructed logic,"[31] I will conclude with two quotations from Marx's "Theses on Feuerbach," which, written in 1845, have a striking sense of foretelling what Garfinkel adopts as his epistemological approach.

The question whether objective truth can be attributed to human thinking is not a question of theory, but is a *practical* question. Man must prove the truth, i.e., the reality and power, the this-sidedness of his thinking in practice. The dispute over the reality or non-reality of thinking that is isolated from practice is a purely *scholastic* question.

All social life is essentially *practical*. All mysteries which lead theory to mysticism find their rational solution in human practice and in the comprehension of this practice.[32]

Ethnomethodology as Phenomenology

In his doctoral dissertation, Garfinkel sets up an analytical distinction between two modes of theorizing that proves to be a useful foundation upon which to view the directions his later works take.[33] The distinction is between "correspondence theory" and "congruence theory."[34]

Correspondence theory is that which claims that there is an essential difference between "the perceived object of the 'outer world' and the concrete object," and that "the concreteness of the object in this view is a property of the object; such concreteness being independent of the various modes, attending of an experiencer. . . . It is in this sense "actual."[35] This type of theory, therefore, is to be seen as positing the existence of a world sui generis.

To the extent that correspondence theory claims a separation between a real world of objects "out there" and the subjective interpretation of that world by individuals, it calls for methodologies (the "canons of logico-empirical inquiry") which attempt the accurate measurement, depiction and reproduction of such "realities" and "objects." Also, the distinction suggested between subject and object requires that these theories offer a version of the *relationship* that exists between the two.[36] We typically see correspondence theories that detail the nature of the relatedness of the subject to the object system by disclosing "tendencies of patterned treatments" of the former to the latter.[37]

As an example of correspondence theory with all its limitations, Garfinkel cites the work of Parsons (whom he otherwise pays homage to as a teacher and adviser). Parsons' sociology is seen as limited by the necessity it imposes upon itself to explain the nature of the relationship between the subject and the object it reifies as a "social system."[38] Such problematic features as a "common value system" are the consequences of this effort.

Garfinkel's preference is for congruence theory. He defines this as a perspective wherein it is maintained that, "The perceived object of the 'outer world' is the concrete object, and that the two terms, 'perceived object' and 'concrete object' are synonymous and interchangeable terms.[39] Furthermore, "The concreteness of the object in this view is found in the object constituted as a unity of meanings and only as a unity of meanings."[40] Garfinkel's exemplar for congruence theory, and the source of much of his later formulations as ethnomethodology is the constitutive phenomenology of Alfred Schutz.[41] In his attempts at synthesizing the works of Weber and Husserl, Schutz delineates the union of subject in terms of phenomenology of the common sense environment. Rather than Parsons' perspective of, "How *can* we believe our eyes," Schutz questions "How *do* we believe our eyes."[42] His answer is in terms of the constitutive features of everyday activities such that they form an "attitude of daily life" that provides members with a manageable view of reality. This view of reality is not in terms of larger social or historical structures and processes but in terms of the here and now of immediate and personal concerns of members. Members operate within "zones of relevance in which they transform incoming objective data into a more usable and personal "stock-of-knowledge-at hand."[43]

Borrowing, in part, from Husserl, Schutz identifies those constitutive features that go into the production of a "world known in common and taken for granted." First, there are "background expectancies"[44] by which the individual assumes, assumes that other individuals assume also, and assumes that people assume about each other such things as (1) that they will take things as they appear to be "as matters of fact" or "objective necessity" and will typically disregard personal interpretations of things not being as they appear to be, (2) that what appears as "actual" for persons will appear the same for any other persons taking their place as witnesses, and (3) that persons recognizing a disparity between the publicly accepted appearance of things and their own personal interpretation of what appears to be will ordinarily withhold giving evidences of such disparities. By attending to such background expectancies Schutz draws attention to the way in which persons manage a *sense* of a reality "out there" and share this sense with others. Operating with common understandings of how the world is to be perceived and communicated to others makes "society possible" for each member. Garfinkel calls such background expectancies the "seen but unnoticed background of common understandings."[45]

Another important element adopted from Schutz (out of Husserl) is Garfinkel's use of the property of "indexicality." Indexicality refers to the reflexive property of language and meanings conveyed through language such that a word or phrase is meaningful in the context or situation in which it is used and loses its meaning out of context. Not only is the word dependent on the context but the context is dependent on the word in that the word is constitutive of, stands for, "indexes" the meaningful features of the context. The word then is a "stand-in" for the "deeper structures"[46] of meaning that run through situations. But in order that simple words or phrases be seen as conveying whole meaning structures, the individual must be seen as an encoding and decoding device. Each item of talk is encoded with much more meaning than the mere words display and each individual is (to the extent that he is competent) capable of "getting" "whatever" is conveyed in talk.[47] Doing encoding and decoding involves practices whereby individuals who trust that others reciprocally trust in the "ordinary aspects" of the situation read a communication for more than it only says to them. "Hello, how are you?", ordinarily elicits responses like, "Fine; how are you?"—not responses like, "How is what part/aspect of me?" Garfinkel calls such practices of reading into—or *creatively* decoding talk or rules for procedure "glossing."[48] We will deal more fully with these and other features when I discuss the invariant aspects in the exchange of communication and in interaction.

Garfinkel suggests, in his doctoral dissertation, the direction his later works will take with respect to these features (e.g., background expectancies and indexicality) as they constitute elements in a model of man. He adopts as a term with a particular emphasis the word "Role," with a capitalized "R".[49] "Role," as distinct from "role," refers to "cognitive style, attitude, mode of attending" as these features are seen to depict the perceptual and cognitive work of members in situations. In addition, and again borrowing from Schutz,[50] Garfinkel claims that "Role" is made up of certain *invariant features* that include the form of sociality, the mode of giveness of the self, the mode of time consciousness, the epoche, the mode of attention to life, and the form of spontaneity.[51] We will merely note these here, reserving them for more detailed discussion later.

Another important source for Garfinkel is the sociology of knowledge of Karl Mannheim.[52] It is from Mannheim that Garfinkel gets the essence of his methodology and another substantive rendition of the relationship between subject and object. Mannheim offers Garfinkel a way of getting at the deeper structures and patterns of meaning carried through contexts and then indexed by evidences such as utterances. This "documentary method" points to the mutual determination of these underlying patterns and their evidences-in-appearances. By treating the reference of an appearance or "sign" as a "document" of, or as "pointing" to the underlying structure or pattern, a link is established between the pattern and its evidences. Not only this, but also the evidences are interpreted on the basis of "what we know" about the pattern underlying them. Thus, appearances and underlying essences are seen to be mutually determinative and supportive, and when taken together, constitute a world of common sense understanding. Garfinkel, for example, uses the phrase, "Isn't that just like Harry," to portray how the unity of a biography is seen and realized by the documentary nature of this phrase such that it provides for both an underlying pattern (Harry is typically like this) and a specific sign (this is something we might expect from Harry).[53] The result of everyday documenting by members is that they come to realize a sense of a continuity of a meaningful reality. Or, to use Garfinkel's words, "The product of the actor's use of the documentary method is the constancy of relationships between an actor and his changing scenes of activity."[54]

We see that through his use of the ideas of Husserl, Schutz and Mannheim, Garfinkel clearly places his own work in the traditions that treat the constituent everyday features of communication and interaction as phenomena in their own right, and just as (if not more) worthy of study as the more structural and institutional properties of man's social world.

In the next section, we will more closely examine these phenomena with the intention of portraying them (as I think Garfinkel does) as invariant, trans-situational, context-free features of everyday life exchanges of communication.

INVARIANT PROPERTIES

By and large the search for and the decision about the invariant elements of action represents a task that has been and remains a strange one to American sociology.[55]

Garfinkel's programmatic intent may be viewed as an effort at correcting what he sees as the inadequacies of prior attempts at dealing with the "invariant elements of action."[56] He suggests that a specific and "leading policy" of ethnomethodology

> is to refuse serious consideration to the prevailing proposal that efficiency, efficacy, effectiveness, intelligibility, consistency, planfulness, typicality, uniformity, reproducibility of activities—i.e., that rational properties of practical activities—be assessed, recognized, categorized, described by using a rule or standard *obtained outside actual settings* within which such properties are recognized, used, produced, and talked about by settings' members.[57]

For Garfinkel, to look "outside" of context for invariant features of social action is to impose arbitrarily often unrealistic and biased versions of what is actually going on. It is only by attending to the *actual features* of the situation that an understanding of social processes can be derived. Of prior interest above and beyond all else among these features is the *universality of consciousness*. Garfinkel's ethnomethodology sees evidence for such universality in the invariant, trans-situational, atemporal family of practices of members active in situations. In this section, I will examine some of these features and practices.

Members are to be seen as recreating "from scratch" a new and uniquely fitted "understanding" for each new and unique situation. This "occasioned corpus"[58] consists of two aspects: first are the contextual data drawn from the specific situation itself; and, second, are a family of "properties of practical reasoning" of an invariant and trans-situational nature.[59] Members are thus seen as drawing from two reserves for the constituting of their understandings; one of the immediacy of the situation and one of universal properties of the structuring of consciousness. Among the latter are such practices as[60] (1) members' assumption of a mutuality and reciprocity of determinations and perspectives on events such that the same sense might be assigned to these events by different witnesses; (2) members' awareness that language is determinative of meanings and that all members share in "a socially standardized process" for the use of talk in constructing meanings; (3) members' tacit acceptance of normal forms, or a "relationship of undoubted correspondence" between things-as-represented and things-as-they-really-are; (4) members' understanding of a continuity in the determination of events such that what is intended now has a history and future of intendedness; and (5) member's recognition that talk, either spoken language or written rules, is never adequate or complete enough to encompass all that an event means for witnesses, and that the repair of such inadequacies by members will involve "glossing techniques," such as "et cetera," "let it pass" and "unless."[61]

These and other related practices have the following qualities: (1) they are assumed by members who assume that other members also assume them and that members ordinarily assume them about each other; (2) they are "seen but unnoticed" qualities for members which, under most conditions, must be breached or violated to come clear; and (3) they are "invariant to the contents of actual descriptions to which they may be attached."[62]

Garfinkel's program, then, is to search for the rules, the invariances, the universals, of the assemblage and disassemblage of each "occasioned corpus." In an early paper, he alludes to the technique he will later expand for this search.[63] Garfinkel speaks of a "praxeological rule"[64] and describes it as

> the search for similarities of successful methods in many different domains of activity. It seeks to formulate statements of method, and to extend their generality, seeking as wide a domain of applicability as possible . . . .
> The use of the praxeological rule has the virtue of drawing attention away from the search for impersonal 'causal lines' of human action, framed in terms of the determinants of an effect, in favor of stating the operations that an investigator conceives the actor to be performing upon a system of relationships to produce the state the sociologist is interested in.[65]

What Garfinkel has accomplished with such a program is to effectively bracket interaction and communication from any institutional and ideational contexts. Nothing outside of the constitutive features counts in the determination of what is going on.

Also bracketed outside of context are personal biography and personal ego. Borrowing from Schutz who is seen as dismissing "subjective states" because of their implication that there *is* a difference between subject and object,[66] Garfinkel takes as constitutive of identity only "the grounds as well as the behavior that the grounds make explicable as the other person's conduct."[67] He suggests

> All talk of an 'Essential' actor, the *real* personality is here rejected. We conceive of an actor as egoless. That a set of experiences are unified in meaning is to be accounted for by stating the conditions in terms of other experiences under which a unity will be found and not by invoking the principle of a unifier . . . . *Analytically,* the term means nothing else than the stream of experience *in process.*[68]

Garfinkel leaves the actor no essential self to fall back on—no autonomous ego into which to draw. How then does the individual "tie" himself together and achieve a maintenance of self from situation to situation? Garfinkel suggests that we achieve *personal invariance* and a sense of a homogenous self by means of an application of the "documentary method"[69] by which "the self— as a homogenous product for other persons, is the outcome of continual and careful management."[70]

The reality of self is thus seen as the result of constitutive practices of actors.

> Whole orders of actions and personnel are treated by the actor under the critically important aspect of 'the sameness of the scene,' i.e. its comparability to situations known in the past, despite the variability of behavioral appearances and the continual alteration of props and scenery. The product of the actor's use of the documentary method is the constancy of relationships between an actor and his changing scenes of activity.[71]

The method consists of treating an actual appearance as 'the document of' as 'pointing to,' as 'standing on behalf of' a presupposed underlying pattern. Not only is the underlying pattern derived from documentary evidences, but the individual documentary evidences in their turn are interpreted on the basis of 'what is known' about the underlying pattern. Each is used to elaborate the other.[72]

Thus, like Goffman's dramaturgy, the self is seen as inextricably tied to the situation—the context. However, unlike Goffman, Garfinkel (1) presupposes no objectified, intersubjectively shared reality as arena for self—there is nothing apart from the constitutive practices of actors (Goffman posits a "rule constituted" order *in which* actors perform with greater or lesser coherence, competence and believability); (2) claims that "management techniques" that enable the actor to leave the "authentic" world and dabble in "impressing" others are not possible—we cannot leave authenticity;[73] and (3) claims the existence of a *universality of consciousness* that comes before the world of appearances and expressions and is constituted by *invariant* properties of practical reasoning.

The use of documenting also points to the universal nature of social behavior such that it involves an exchange of trust and a tacit understanding to suspend critical judgment of "what is going on." The documentary method is "intimately related to the phenomenon of trust. Through the documentary method, persons are enabled to trust such properties of a scene as invariants despite continual alterations of actual appearances."[74] The consequence is a *sense* of a social structure and a *sense* of an order repeatedly enacted from moment to moment and dependent upon what members "understand" as background expectancies.

While Garfinkel does not allow the actor an essential self he does maintain the existence of some constitutive factors in the determination of what actors come to be and how actors might be seen in their activities. But these factors are far from the type of things that would allow for the distinctiveness of one actor as compared to others—in fact, Garfinkel again speaks of these as invariant and universal features. Derived from Schutz, they appear in Garfinkel's work[75] as

1. *the form of sociality,* by which is meant the nature of I–thou and I–me relationships in that the thou or me serve as "interpretive schemes . . . or . . . standards for identifying or defining the other person or the self";[76]
2. *giveness of the self,* or "a set of memories that are selected and made relevant by an attitudinal me so as to specify a me in the world";[77]
3. *the epoche,* by which is meant a selective process or "procedural rule whereby a class or classes of possibilities are removed from the operations of judgment and are treated within the conditions of this abstention";[78]
4. *attention to life,* or "an attitude of interest or no interest in meeting, elaborating, and/or testing the consequent possibilities of experience that are immanently proposed in and through the experience of a field of objects";[79]
5. *time consciousness,* by which Garfinkel means the structuring of time relative to an object and the "time of experience of the object relative to other objects";[80]
6. *form of spontaneity,* which refers to "the principle, teleological or expressional, that governs the course of activity,"[81] that is, the stance that makes activity be seen as meaningful with reference to a pre-conceived project or a projected plan. It is the quality of the form of spontaneity that activity is experienced as a "now."

With these six constitutive features Garfinkel has completed his elaboration of the *trans-situational, atemporal, universal* qualities of the everyday attitude and cognitive style of members. By their use Garfinkel intends to display,

that there stands in the static stream of experiences an *invariant interpretive scheme* . . . By the term invariant we mean that the interpretive scheme is not affected in its meanings by the fluctuations of intention and object found in the staticized flow of experience.[82]

In the next section, I will examine the dynamic that results from members with members' interpretive schemes converging. I will suggest that what results is a process of negotiation by which an *exchange of communication* takes place. Such exchange will be seen as constitutive of members' assessment and realization of a reality held in common and taken for granted.

CONCLUSION: AN EXCHANGE OF COMMUNICATION

The policy is recommended that any social setting be viewed as self-organizing with respect to the intelligible character of its own appearances as either representations of or as evidences-of-a-social-order . . . .
Structurally differing organized practical activities of everyday life are to be sought out and examined for the production, origins, recognition, and respresentations of rational practices. All 'logical' and 'methodological' properties of action, every feature of an activity's sense, facticity, objectively, accountability, communicality is to be treated as *a contingent accomplishment of socially organized communication practices.*[83]

The issues of ethnomethodology are the issues of communication exchange in that the ethnomethodological search is for the communication processes that lead to a sense of common understanding among people. The uniqueness of ethnomethodology's concerns is the recognition that such understanding when it occurs is not a consequence of factors external to or antecedent to an event (e.g., norms, authority, biography, psychological need), but rather entails "an 'inner' temporal course of interpretive work."[84] "The world is essentially without meaning;"[85] and, for members of that world meaning or understanding is obtainable only through processes of creation. Ethnomethodology is concerned with the *creation* of meaning and the *sharing* of this meaning among members.

Since there is no meaning, and, hence, no reality "out there" waiting to be uncovered, any "sense" of reality is to be seen as the consequence of members' "work" in each new situation. The nature of this "work" or the "practical actions" of members is that it is problematic, i.e., it is not assured, certain or preordained.[86] Rather, it is an intricate process of negotiation-in-context among members in which claims are made, essences identified, meanings suggested, and realities proposed such that what is identified, suggested and proposed is to be taken as what "really" is going on. Members are, thus, to be seen as engaged in the attempted production of "facts." To the extent that something will be seen as factual, it will have met the test of acceptance. Ethnomethodology is concerned with the practices employed by members to ensure the factual nature of their claims, and to see and accept other members' claims as factual. In all of this the production of meaning, understanding and facts is to be viewed as a practical accomplishment of members, and the sharing of meaning, understanding and a sense of the factual is to be viewed as consequent to a process of an exchange of communication.

Garfinkel uses the term, "accounts," to refer to members' attempts to capture this sense of reality.[87] An account is a linguistic device for making "sense" out of a situation, and for communicating this sense in ordinary, understandable, and rational terms. The communication of accountably rational versions of reality thus becomes the work of interaction, and members employ various practices to accomplish this:

> . . . the practices consist of members' methods for assembling sets of alternatives, members' methods for assembling, testing and verifying the factual character of information, members' methods for giving an account of circumstances of choice and choices, members' methods for assessing, producing, recognizing, insuring, and enforcing consistency, coherence, effectiveness, efficiency, planfulness, and other rational properties of individual and concerted actions.[88]

What makes the doing of accounts particularly interesting is that those who do them apparently work just as hard at *not seeing* the ad hoc constitutive nature of their practices, but rather treat their and others' accounts as *actual* and *factual* renditions of reality. Members do this because they are ruled by a feature "of such singular and prevailing relevance that it controls other features in their specific character . . ." that is, that " . . . members take for granted that a member must at the outset *'know'* the settings in which he is to operate . . ."[89] What is entailed in "knowing" are members' reasonable practices, plausible arguments and reportable accountable communications such that these practices involve a *trust among members in the tacit acceptance of a taken-for-granted-reality.* To do otherwise would be "to make the 'reflexive' character of practical activities observable . . .[and] . . . like members wherever they engage in practical sociological inquiries: though they would, they *can* have none of it."[90] For, to make practical activities "observable," and to get behind the practices that make meaning and reality, is to make such meaning and reality "strange" (to bracket it) and, thus, to lose it.

Accounts are thus seen as the *methods and the substance* of doing meaningful and rationally reportable communication of reality. Accounts are viewed as ever-developing within situations, and as they thus *describe* the situation they are seen as being described *by* the situation. Garfinkel displays this dynamic reflexivity in an analysis (account) of a husband and wife communicating.[91]

HUSBAND: Dana succeeded in putting a penny in a parking meter today without being picked up.	*This afternoon as I was bringing Dana, our four-year-old son, home from the nursery school, he succeeded in reaching high enough to put a penny in a parking meter when we parked in a meter parking zone, whereas before he has always had to be picked up to reach that high.*
WIFE: Did you take him to the record store?	*Since he put a penny in a meter that means that you stopped while he was with you. I know that you stopped at the record store either on the way to get him or on the way back. Was it on the way back, so that he was with you or did you stop there on the way to get him and somewhere else on the way back?*

HUSBAND: No, to the shoe repair shop.	*No, I stopped at the record store on the way to get him and stopped at the shoe repair shop on the way home when he was with me.*
WIFE: What for?	*I know of one reason why you might have stopped at the shoe repair shop. Why did you in fact?*
HUSBAND: I got some new shoe laces for my shoes.	*As you will remember I broke a shoe lace on one of my brown oxfords the other day so I stopped to get some new laces.*
WIFE: Your loafers need new heels badly.	*Something else you could have gotten that I was thinking of. You could have taken in your black loafers which need heels badly. You'd better get them taken care of pretty soon.*

What is evident in this account is the nature of the exchange of communication such that it reveals the following:[92] (1) exchanges of communication ordinarily involve more substance than is expressed in words—such substance is understood by members; (2) that which is understood rests upon "unspoken" factors and not on the actual elements of talk; (3) that which is understood often is a result of the use that members make of the temporal and sequential nature of talk such that what is earlier spoken may serve as "documentary evidence" of that conversation which later develops. Communication thus is seen as having a retrospective–prospective sense to it; (4) common understanding results from the tacit acceptance by members of talk as standing for, the document of an underlying meaning each supposes the other grasps. (Thus underlying meaning is reflexively tied to the talk such that each supports, documents the other.); (5) members in communication exchanges utilize and recognize that others utilize current contexts, "biography," and "prospects" for interpreting and giving meaning to each element of talk that occurs; and (6) knowing this, members ordinarily wait for closures and completions in communications in order to make sense of what has come before.[92]

The sense of all this is that the outcome of conversation, or exchanges of communication, is to be seen not as a consequence of factors external to the exchange (such as need, motive, intent) but as an operation going on *within* the exchange itself. Meaning, therefore, is not *imposed*, but is *constituted* through members' practical accomplishments.[93]

Since occasions and their sense are to be seen as practical accomplishments, this presents members (and sociologists viewing members) with an essential difficulty. How are they to distinguish in actual occasions between those which are merely "indexical expressions" (those whose "sense" is subjectively and often arbitrarily linked to context) and "objective expressions" (those to be seen as actual, literal transcriptions of what-really-is-going-on)? Garfinkel suggests that this task is paramount in the scheme of members' everyday activities. They attempt to meet it with such procedures as "formulations," "glosses" and "documentations."

A "formulation" is a procedure whereby a member "describes," "explains," "translates," "summarizes," "explicates," "furnishes the gist of," "takes note of its accordance with rules," or "remarks on its departure from rules" his own or the communications of others, such that the indexical nature of such communications is seen to be repaired and accountably transformed into objective talk.

> With ubiquitous prevalence and insistence members do formulations as remedies for problematic features that the properties of indexical expressions present to their attempts to satisfy the aims of distinguishing in actual occasions between objective and indexical expressions, and, in actual occasions, providing objective expressions as substitutes for indexicals.[94]

To "formulate," then, is to talk about talk, to string along with utterances a series of subtitles that explicate the sense of talk-in-process. Such formulations as, "in other words," "as we all know," "that is" and "in the end" serve to locate individual talks with an underlying essence of what they mean and where they stand.

"Glossing" is a related procedure for a short cut in the process of communicating understanding and meaning. A gloss may be the "et cetera," "unless" or "let it pass" of common conversations— else it may be the "positivism," "in God we trust," or "Britannia rules the seas" of broader concerns.[95] In each case, the gloss constitutes a *rule* by which individual (and otherwise) unique events, utterances, exchanges take on a precoded sense of meaning. To the extent that members share and mutually accept the sense of meaning a gloss represents, we may say that they have common understanding and, thus, their exchanges of communication will be facilitated.

To "document" is: (1) to search for and determine the underlying pattern of meaning indexically reflected by events or talk; (2) to treat such talk as part of, and motivated by, an intended sense of action; and (3) to employ retrospective-progressive readings of present events, talk and occurrences to "maintain the indexicality of the object through temporal and circumstantial alterations."[96] To quote Garfinkel, "Such method seems to be an inextricable feature of situations in which the rules that govern communicative exchanges create situations in which actions must be taken despite the fact of incomplete information."[97]

Garfinkel would maintain that since *no* situation is completely covered by rules for "communicative exchanges" (the situation of the man-in-the-street or the scientist-in-the-laboratory), *all* members in *all* situations employ documentary methods for practical theorizing to ferret out and to communicate the sense of what is going on.

We see then that Garfinkel's ethnomethodology is indeed a study of the exchange of communication. By bracketing the very processes of talk, he has depicted, in unique and revealing ways, how individuals, in spite of, apart from—and yet, paradoxically, often in relation to the contexts in which they live—create, sustain and exchange meaningful communication. Understanding is thus seen as resulting not only from verbally transmitted meanings but also non-verbally through the tacit knowledge and invariant structures that go into the make-up of verbal communication. The "rules" of interpretation Garfinkel proposes act as a "common value system" presupposing the possibility of shared meanings and accountably rational communication exchanges.[98] In this sense what Garfinkel introduces is a "normative" orientation on a level that sociology has not really given much attention—that is, the invariant and universal properties of communication.

NOTES

1. Along with Attewell, we see ethnomethodology as a separate and unique paradigm because of its "commitment to study universals." See Paul Attewell, "Ethnomethodology Since Garfinkel," in *Theory and Society* 1 (1974), pp. 179–210; see, especially, pp. 207–208. I would however, disagree with Attewell's contention that Garfinkel "lacks the commitment to invariance which characterized the later ethnomethodologists (p. 205). This erroneous claim appears to result from a dependence on *Studies in Ethnomethodology*, (Englewood Cliffs, N.J.: Prentice-Hall, 1967) for a total perspective on Garfinkel. I would recommend that such a misconception might be easily remedied by an examination of Garfinkel's "Perception of the Other" (unpublished Ph.D. dissertation, Harvard University, 1952).
2. See, for example, H. Sacks, "Sociological Description." *Berkeley Journal of Sociology* 8 (1963), pp. 1–17.
3. See, for example, D. Zimmerman and M. Pollner, "The Everyday World as a Phenomenon," (in J. Douglas, ed., *Understanding Everyday Life*, Chicago, Aldine Publishing Company, 1970, pp. 80–103).
4. See, for example: A. Blum, "Theorizing," (in J. Douglas, *Understanding Everyday Life*, pp. 305–323), and "The Corpus of Knowledge as a Normative Order," in J. McKinney and E. Tiryakian, eds., *Theoretical Sociology: Perspectives and Developments* (New York: Appleton-Century-Crofts, 1970, pp. 319–336); P. McHugh, "On the Failure of Positivism," (in J. Douglas, *Understanding Everyday Life*, pp. 324–335).
5. See, for example: A Cicourel, *Method and Measurement in Sociology* (New York: Free Press, 1964); "Basic and Normative Rules in the Negotiation of Status and Role," in Hans P. Dreitzel, ed., Recent Sociology No. 2 (New York: Macmillan, 1970), pp. 4–45; "The Acquisition of Social Structure: Toward a Developmental Sociology of Language and Meaning," in J. Douglas, *Understanding Everyday Life*, pp. 136–168; "Cross Modal Communication: The Representational Context of Socio-Linguistic Information Processing," Monograph Series on *Language and Linguistics No. 25*, (Georgetown School of Language and Linguistics, 1970), *Cognitive Sociology: Language and Meaning in Social Interaction* (New York: The Free Press, 1974).
6. For example, while Cicourel's *Method and Measurement in Sociology* can certainly be seen as a critique of other sociologies, Garfinkel states that "ethnomethodological studies are not directed to formulating or arguing correctives" *(Studies in Ethnomethodology*, p. viii). For the reaction of a

"conventional sociologist" see Lewis A. Coser, "Two Methods in Search of a Substance," Presidential Address, *American Sociological Review* 40 [6] (December 1975), pp. 691–700. We would maintain that Coser's rejection of ethnomethodology as a viable and important approach is more reflective of Coser's limitations than those of ethnomethodology. His critique reflects basic and extensive misunderstandings of the ethnomethodological approach.

7. Thomas Kuhn, *The Structure of Scientific Revolutions.*
8. K. Marx and F. Engels, *The German Ideology* (New York: International Publishers, 1846, 1947), p. 14.
9. Garfinkel, *Studies in Ethnomethodology.* Other works by Garfinkel include the following: "Perception of the Other;" "Conditions of Successful Degradation Ceremonies," *American Journal of Sociology* 61 (1956), pp. 420–424; "Some Sociological Concepts of Methods for Psychiatrists," *Psychiatric Research Reports* 6 (1956), pp. 181–195; "Aspects of the Problem of Common Sense Knowledge of Social Structures," *Transactions of the Forth World Congress of Sociology* 4 (Milan: Stressa, 1959), pp. 56–65; "Common-Sense Knowledge of Social Structures: The Documentary Method of Interpretation," in J. M. Scher, ed., *Theories of the Mind* (New York: Free Press, 1962), pp. 689–712; "A Conception of, and Experiments with, 'Trust' as a Condition of Stable Concerted Actions," in O. J. Harvey, ed., *Motivation and Social Interaction.* (New York: Ronald Press, 1963), pp. 187–238. "Practical Sociological Reasoning: Some Features in the Work of the Los Angeles Suicide Prevention Center," in E. S. Shneidman, ed., *Essays in Self-Destruction* (New York: Science House, 1967), pp. 171–187; with H. Sacks, "On Formal Structures of Practical Actions," in J. C. McKinney and E. A. Tiryakian, eds., *Theoretical Sociology: Perspectives and Developments,* (New York: Appleton-Century-Crofts, 1970), pp. 337–366.
   Several of Garfinkel's earlier "writings" are dittoed transcriptions of course notes and are difficult, if not impossible, to obtain.
10. Terms such as "utterances" are often substituted for more common usages such as "conversations" or "talk" to stylistically convey the stance of "strangeness" that ethnomethodologists take in relation to ordinary events and phenomena. To treat an event or phenomenon as "strange" is, in Schutz's sense, to "bracket" it from its contexts and treat it as a phenomenon in its own right.
11. But, in another sense, *broadened.*
12. Garfinkel, "Perception of the Other," p. 13 (emphasis added).
13. Garfinkel, *Studies in Ethnomethodology,* p. 24.
14. Garfinkel, "Perception of the Other," p. 383.
15. Garfinkel, "On Formal Structures of Practical Action," pp. 345–346.
16. Ibid., pp. 345–346.
17. Ibid., p. 345–346.
18. Garfinkel, *Studies in Ethnomethodology,* p. 68.
19. While the whole of Garfinkel's work may be seen as relating to the elaboration of this concept, the reader might pay special interest to *Studies in Ethnomethodology* where it receives substantive and varied treatments, and also, "On Formal Structures of Practical Action," especially, pp. 348–350.
20. Garfinkel, "On Formal Structures of Practical Action, p. 349.

21. Ibid., p. 341.
22. See, for example, Norman K. Denzin, "Symbolic Interactionism and Ethnomethodology," in J. Dougals, ed., *Understanding Everyday Life*, pp. 261–286. Also see the Rejoinder by Zimmerman and Wieder, "Ethnomethodology and the Problem of Order: Comment on Denzin," in J. Douglas, pp. 287–302.
23. Karl Marx, *Capital*, vol. I (Moscow, n.d.), p. 20.
24. Ibid., p. 20.
25. Garfinkel, *Studies in Ethnomethodology*, Chapter 4.
26. For a discussion of "literal description" see Thomas P. Wilson, "Normative and Interpretive Paradigms in Sociology," in J. Douglas, pp. 57–79. See, especially, pp. 71–74.
27. See Garfinkel's "A Conception of, and Experiments with, 'Trust' as a Condition of Stable Concerted Actions."
28. Garfinkel, *Studies in Ethnomethodology*, pp. 37–38.
29. Ibid., p. 37–38.
30. Garfinkel, "Practical Sociological Reasoning," p. 178.
31. This term originates with A. Kaplan. See *The Conduct of Inquiry* (San Francisco: Chandler, 1964). Kaplan distinguishes "reconstructed logic" from "logic in use."
32. Marx, "Theses on Feuerback," *Early Writings*, pp. 422–423.
33. Garfinkel, "Perception of the Other," 1952, pp. 93–96.
34. Garfinkel derives these terms from the work of Felix Kaufman. See his *Methodology of the Social Sciences* (New York: Oxford University Press, 1944), especially pp. 95–99.
35. Garfinkel, "Perception of the Other," p. 93.
36. Ibid., p. 141.
37. Ibid.
38. Talcott Parsons, *The Social System* (Glencoe,: Free Press, 1951).
39. Garfinkel, "Perception of the Other," p. 95.
40. Ibid., p. 96.
41. See especially Schutz' papers: "Some Leading Concepts in Phenomenology," *Social Research* 12 (1945), pp. 77–79; "On Multiple Realities," *Philosophical and Phenomenological Research* 4 (1945), pp. 533–75; "Choosing Among Projects of Action," *Philosophical and Phenomenological Research* 12 (1951), pp. 161–84; and, "Common Sense and Scientific Interpretation of Human Action," *Philosophical and Phenomenological Research* 14 (1953), pp. 1–37.

    Schutz' complete works are to be found in "Phenomenology and the Social Sciences," in Marvin Farber, ed., *Philosophical Essays in Memory of Edmund Husserl* (Cambridge, Mass.: Harvard University Press, 1940), pp. 164–186; *Collected Papers I: The Problem of Social Reality*, Maurice Natanson, ed. (The Hague: Martinus Nijihoff, 1962); *Collected Papers II: Studies in Social Theory*, Arvid Broderson, ed. (The Hague: Martinus Nijihoff, 1964); *Collected Papers III: Studies in Phenomenological Philosophy*, I. Schutz, ed. (The Hague: Martinus Nijihoff, 1966).
42. Garfinkel, "Perception of the Other," p. 91.
43. Schutz, *Collected Papers II*, pp. 124–125.
44. See Schutz', "On Multiple Realities" and "Common Sense and Scientific Interpretations of Human Action."

45. Garfinkel, *Studies in Ethnomethodology*, p. 44.
46. For an analysis of "deep structures" see the works of N. Chomsky, e.g., *Aspects of a Theory of Syntax* (Cambridge, Mass.: MIT Press, 1965).
47. For a discussion of members' competence, see *Studies in Ethnomethodology*, p. 57 n.8. See also the various essays (e.g., "Coolness in Everyday Life") in Lyman and Scott, *A Sociology of the Absurd*.

An interesting parallel to the methodological use of indexicality by Garfinkel is the *verstehende soziologie* of Weber. Both theorists reflect a tradition that claims that the methods and concerns of the natural sciences are inappropriate for the study of man's social behavior. For Garfinkel this is represented by his substitution, for any "scientific" measurement, of techniques of *subjectively* "understanding" the contextual features of an event so as to justify seeing a sign as an index of those features. Both the ethnomethodologist and members-as-practical-theorists are seen as *interpreting* by the use of non-scientific procedures a sense of "what is going on here."

Weber inherited this tradition primarily from Wilhelm Dilthey and Heinrich Rickert. Dilthey's work was a direct attack on the positivist orientation of Comte and others to make a "natural science" of sociology. He attempted to forge a different methodology to deal with the uniqueness of the human mind. Proposing *verstehen*, or, subjective interpretation, Dilthey claimed that through "reliving" social events the social scientist could grasp the unique form of human consciousness. "All knowledge is knowledge of experience; but the original unity of all experience and its resulting validity are conditioned by the factors which mould the consciousness within which it arises . . . ." (Dilthey, in Marcello Truzzi, *Verstehen: Subjective Understanding in the Social Sciences* (Reading, Mass.: Addison-Wesley Pub. Co., 1974, p. 10). Rickert expressed some disagreement with Dilthey (e.g., use of the word verstehen); but he also posited the primacy of "meaning" in the attempt to understand human action (Truzzi, p. 19).
48. For an example of glossing see Garfinkel, *Studies in Ethnomethodology*, Chapter 3.
49. Garfinkel, "Perception of the Other," p. 160.
50. Schutz, "On Multiple Realities."
51. See Garfinkel, "Perception of the Other," Chapter 7–12 for a detailed elaboration of these features.
52. See especially "On the Interpretation of Weltenschauung," in Karl Mannheim, *Essays on the Sociology of Knowledge* (New York: Oxford University Press, 1952). See Garfinkel, "Some Sociological Concepts of Methods for Psychiatrists," for a clear elaboration of what he draws from Mannheim.
53. Garfinkel, ibid., pp. 193–194.
54. Ibid., p. 194.
55. Garfinkel, "Perception of the Other," p. 118.
56. I do not intend to portray all of Garfinkel's work as an intended corrective, however to the extent that recognizing a void and seeking to fill it is a remedial action, then Garfinkel can be seen as "correcting" the "strangeness" of the coverage of invariant elements of action in American sociology.
57. Garfinkel, 'Studies in Ethnomethodology, p. 33 (emphasis mine).

58. "Occasioned corpus" is a term coined by Zimmerman and Pollner ("The Everyday World as Phenomenon," in J. Douglas, ed., *Understanding Everyday Life*) to refer to features of social action that are "particular, contingent accomplishments of the production and recognition work of parties to the activity" (p. 44).
59. See, for example, Garfinkel, *Studies in Ethnomethodology*, Chapter 8.
60. The following are derived from Garfinkel's "Aspects of the Problem of Common-Sense Knowledge of Social Structures," and *Studies in Ethnomethodology* Chapter 8, and pp. 55–56.
61. "Glossing" is necessary because of the "looseness" of rules. Garfinkel's discussion of "looseness" is found in "Practical Sociological Reasoning," pp. 177–178.
62. Garfinkel, "Problem of Common Sense Knowledge of Social Structures," p. 54.
63. Garfinkel, "Some Sociological Concepts of Methods for Psychiatrists."
64. Garfinkel adopts this term from Henry Hiz, "Kotarbinski's Praxeology," *Philosophy and Phenomenological Research* (December 1954), pp. 238–243.
65. Garfinkel, "Some Sociological Concepts of Methods for Psychiatrists," pp. 191–192.
66. Garfinkel, "Perception of the Other."
67. Garfinkel, "Conditions of Successful Degradation Ceremonies," p. 420.
68. Garfinkel, "Perception of the Other," pp. 169–170.
69. Garfinkel, "Some Sociological Concepts of Methods for Psychiatrists," p. 194. See also *Studies inEthnomethodology*, p. 78.
70. Garfinkel, "Some Sociological Concepts of Methods for Psychiatrists," p. 194.
71. Ibid., p. 194.
72. Garfinkel, *Studies in Ethnomethodology*, p. 78.
73. For Garfinkel's criticisms of Goffman on this point see *Studies in Ethnomethodology*, pp. 165–180.
74. Garfinkel, "Some Sociological Concepts of Methods for Psychiatrists," p. 194.
75. Garfinkel, "Perception of the Other," Chapters 7–12.
76. Ibid., p. 164.
77. Ibid., p. 413. A related set of conceptualizations is to be found in Klapper's discussion of selective exposure, selective perception and selective retention. See J. Klapper, *The Effects of Mass Communication* (New York: Free Press, 1965), pp. 19–26.
78. Garfinkel, Ibid., p. 416.
79. Ibid., p. 417.
80. Ibid., p. 420.
81. Ibid., p. 422.
82. Ibid., pp. 171–172 (emphasis added).
83. Garfinkel, *Studies in Ethnomethodology*, p. 33.
84. Ibid., p. 31.
85. Lyman and Scott, *A Sociology of the Absurd*, p. 1.
86. Garfinkel, *Studies in Ethnomethodology*, p. 31.
87. See for example, Garfinkel, "On Formal Structures of Practical Actions," p. 342.
88. Ibid., p. 342.

89. Garfinkel, *Studies in Ethnomethodology*, p. 8. (emphasis added).
90. Ibid., p. 9.
91. The following colloquy is found in ibid., pp. 38–39.
92. Adapted from ibid., pp. 39–40.
93. In this regard there is a similarity between Goffman and Garfinkel with respect to their views of the individual. For both he would appear to be involved in a drama in which a good actor is one who is capable of mustering impressionarily (in the case of Goffman) and linguistically (in the case of Garfinkel) convincing accounts.
94. Garfinkel, "On Formal Structures of Practical Actions," pp. 350–353.
95. Garfinkel, *Studies in Ethnomethodology*, pp. 20–21.
96. Garfinkel, "Some Sociological Concepts of Methods for Psychiatrists," p. 195.
97. Ibid., p. 195.
98. An interesting line of criticism (intentional or otherwise) of Garfinkel's "interpretive rules" may be found in the works of Dreitzel ("Introduction" to *Recent Sociology* No. 2); Jurgen Habermas (e.g., "Some Distinctions in Universal Pragmatics," in Theory and Society, Vol. 3, No. 2, 1976); and Trent Schroyer ("Toward a Critical Theory for Advanced Industrial Society," in Dreitzel).

These authors challenge the sense of interpretive rules, claiming instead that such rules may in fact be seen as deriving from thoroughly *non-creative* arenas such as power, technology and class struggles, and that a preoccupation with an interpretive paradigm is a delusion: if the norms of social interaction are but crystallizations of power relations and work situations, they obviously cannot be the result of accounting procedures (Dreitzel, pp. xviii–xix).

S I X : : A Theoretical Resolution : Society as Exchange

CRITICAL SUMMARY OF THE PROGRAM AND SUBSTANCE OF THE STUDY AND A THEORETICAL RESOLUTION OF THE PROBLEM

In the introduction, I suggested that social exchange theory, a perspective which draws some considerable attention in contemporary sociology, is fraught with basic theoretical, epistemological and methodological difficulties.[1] Central among these are (1) a general tendency, often linked to such specifics as biological drives, psychological needs, and economic processes, of emphasizing to exclusivity those processes of human social behavior exemplified by a fairly rational working out of non-problematic properties; (2) a persistent inability of exchange theory to deal successfully with the emergent properties of institutional and structural societal qualities; and (3) an inability at identifying universal and invariant properties of sufficient credibility to yield a comprehensive theory of social behavior.

Our general position is this. While I feel in agreement with the generic qualities of the exchange mechanism as illustrative of the dynamics of social behavior, I do not agree with the various premises on which it has been grounded. Biological drives, psychological needs and economic non-problematics do not appear to us to be sufficient as bases for a comprehensive application of the general exchange mechanism.

We have argued in this study for a critical perspective that would serve to identify the weaknesses and limitations of that which is termed exchange theory. And, we have suggested that the redeemable qualities of the exchange model would benefit from the addition of correctives drawn from Goffman's dramaturgical analysis and Garfinkel's ethnomethodology. These two perspectives were selected because of the promise they displayed at the outset for providing unique and substantive answers to the questions raised by the inadequacies of conventional exchange theory as typified in the writings of Homans and Blau.

While much of our attention has been directed toward a programmatic, point-by-point working-out of the difficulties with social exchange theory through the inclusion of new "voices" in the chorus, we are mindful of the need for a more cohesive integration of various "improvements." The present section will suggest such an integration and in doing so proposes a theoretical resolution to the problems previously identified with social exchange. We will begin by first summarizing the contributions of Homans and Blau, building from there.

Homans sets the tone for our investigations by proposing to unearth the basic and elementary properties of human social behavior. His purpose is to explain social action in ways that will bring to the surface such "starting properties" as are universally applicable to all situations of social interaction. Early influence from Pareto suggested to him that the primary building blocks of a theoretical understanding of behavior are to be sought among such non-logical elements as sentiments, appetities, impulses and states of mind. However, Pareto is unable to provide Homans with a manner of getting at such elements other than in ways which treat their symptoms or manifestations in residues. Homans required a clearer, more approachable path to the basic and elementary properties he sought; this path was partially begun for him by the work of Murray. Murray provided Homans with a link between the type of unapproachable psychological needs and sentiments he had discovered in Pareto and a more empirically defensible class of viscerogenic or biological needs. Murray's needs provide the background and even the causal bases from which to view such social psychological properties as sentiment, appetites and states of mind. Armed with these empirical linkages and the supposition that people ordinarily will seek to satisfy the various forms their needs take, Homans next sets out in pursuit of a deductive program that will pull together needs-as-forms and needs-as-dynamics so as to produce an explanation of human social behavior in the form of causally linked propositions. Along the way he pauses occasionally to sharpen his theoretical claws on the bastions of cultural anthropology and structural-functionalism, both of which he maintains are profiteering on false conceptions of what true explanation of social behavior ought to be. Homans' complaint is that, unlike his own orientation, these perspectives are not much interested in basic causes, rather, they claim to be doing explanation by an ex post facto look into effects. This, says Homans, cannot possibly produce an empirically defensible claim to anything beyond the theorist's own biases.

Homans' cultivation of a deductive system of explanation begins to flower with his discovery of Skinnerian behaviorism. In Skinner he discovers an observable and testable motif for the development of variable properties of those basic elements he could until now merely offer descriptively. With the aid of the tenets of operant conditioning Homans feels he is able to get to the *why* of human behavior in a methodologically and theoretically defensible fashion. The fruit of this discovery is the beginning of the modern variant of social exchange theory.

Homans' exchange theory of human social behavior contains nothing esoteric or terribly sophisticated—Homans, himself, often comments that he offers little more than what is otherwise immediately intelligible as common sense. It is suggested that people seek that which is rewarding in their lives and attempt to avoid that which is punishing and that a program of some specificity can be derived which presents the outcomes of various contingencies of reward/punishment conditions. Such a program is premised primarily on the tenets of operant conditioning and a tacit acceptance of a class of psycho-social needs (e.g., acceptance, liking, approval, consonance with the group) which, it is suggested, are basic to the human make-up. Having identified the basic elements and basic dynamics, Homans need only stand back and observe the meanderings of men as they are propelled by an assumed rationality of the pursuit of need-satisfaction.

The only complication in this seemingly logical working out of the non-logical is the eventuality of a conflict between individuals whose pursuit of need-satisfactions clash. Homans has several seemingly neat solutions to this condition. One is that the satisfactions of an individual's seeking of rewards should be commensurate with what he "invests." The rule of "distributive justice" settles conflicting claims for rewards by imposing a preordained hierarchy that specifies who is most worthy and deserving.

Conflicting claims are also, and most typically, settled by means of basic elements of exchange behavior. Recognizing the unlikelihood of achieving all that they seek, men generally enter into negotiations and bargainings with other men in a manner which resembles a marketplace barter. In subtle and not so subtle ways men exchange aspects of their mutually exclusive advantages over one another so that each derives some measure of that which he seeks, while at the same time each is instrumental in the other achieving some measure of his interests. Social life then is to be seen as a mutuality of satisfactions deriving from a fairly unproblematic working out of an assumed rationality of needs. And social exchange is, here, seen as the essential dynamic in that it is any behavior that is motivated by the expectation of return from others. Such return is to be seen as within a realm of acceptibility for each member.

Homans' exchange theory of social behavior makes some notable contributions toward the development of a comprehensive theory of society and social behavior. First of all it clearly depicts man as an active agent with his own interests and goals and a programmatic orientation toward achieving them. Second, it portrays the process of social behavior as essentially a negotiation leading toward certain intended outcomes. Third, as a cognitive psychology it depicts and tacitly emphasizes the subjective, evaluative processes of actors. And, fourth, it offers a foundation and a contribution to an identification and categorization of the needs and need-states which very well may be determinative of man's social behavior. Homans, then, has given us both an understanding of "causes," and the dynamics of exchange that provide for the working out of such causes as constitutive of human social behavior.

Homans' scheme however, is by itself not complete enough to stand on its own as a comprehensive theory of society. Its most notable deficiencies and limitations derive from the fact that it is unable to meaningfully account for the emergence of the more complex properties and structures of societies. Homans' exchange theory works best when it restricts itself to two member direct exchange. Based as it is on properties of a reductionist psychology it cannot adequately deal with the more objectified and institutional arenas of social behavior. Such factors as power, authority, domination, exploitation, inequality and stratification are not accounted for by a theory that goes scarcely beyond the need-driven aspects of human behavior. What is needed as corrective is some connection between what men seeking need-satisfaction do with regard to other men with other need-drives—and the larger institutional manifestations of the outcomes of such an elementary process.

Peter Blau attempts such a connection. Blau is critical of the reductionism in Homans' theory because of its imposition of limitations at producing an analysis of levels of complex structures. Blau sets out to mediate between this type of reductionism and those "grand theories" that do attempt an analysis of complex structures yet which pay little heed to the activities of men as men.

The crucial and connecting links Blau offers between elementary and complex processes and structures are those inevitable consequences resultant from the typical asymmetry of of exchange relationships. Exchange, for Blau, is rarely done under conditions where each member has offerings equal to those of each other member. Some of this inequality is negotiable through a lopsided distribution of whatever might be the medium (goods, capital, aid or information) involved in the exchange. Often, however, the nature of the value inequality of offerings is so great that he who offers less cannot possibly reciprocate in kind. In such situations the slack is taken up by the lesser paying the greater in such coins as deference, obedience, loyalty or submission. What Blau suggests, then, is that a *natural* consequence of exchange is the deriving by some of various forms of power over others.

Inequalities of power distribution may, in some instance, be sufficient for explaining emergent structures of a more complex order (rule by demagogy may be of this class). However, Blau is not satisfied with the exercise of power *per se*, as a *sole* explanation of emergent structures; there are sufficient examples of instances where power exercised has little, if anything to do with the emergent properties of a social order. Blau's corrective is to introduce a "norm of fairness," which, derived from the actual history of the activity of men and not assumed *a priori*, serves as an evaluative base from which men adjudge fair or unfair the exercise of power resultant from asymmetrical exchanges. Power manifestly adjudged fair engenders compliance to an order seen as legitimate, while power adjudged unfair may result in opposition and resistance. What Blau introduces with this conception is a social ethic of trust and morality—indeed, a normative order. It is, then, a fairly easy transition to go from elementary economic-based exchanges to complex forms of a higher order.

Blau, then, unlike Homans, is seen to provide for an extension of exchange theory from the confines of two-person direct exchanges to indirect, generalized exchange at the level of whole social orders. This, however useful as it may be at more fully developing a comprehensive theory of society, is not yet sufficient in and of itself for such attainment. Blau, much like Homans, makes an assumption which presents a serious limitation on any possible application of his version of exchange as a comprehensive theory of society. For both Blau and Homans the social world is depicted as an arena in which interaction is accomplished through processes possessed of an assumed rationality (for Homans, the determinism of drives and needs; for Blau, the determinism of the pursuit of self-interest gain through economics); an arena, that is, which apart from the exigencies of "doing" need-satisfaction or economics is otherwise seen as unproblematic. Men are portrayed as attaining measures of achievement or non-achievement of goals as these outcomes are seen to result from processes possessed of certain rational properties. The focus is on outcomes, probabilities of repeating acts previously rewarded, and the working out of an economics of self-interest presumably held fast by actors certain of the directions they take. Little, if any, mention is made of outcomes of uncertainty, the *pursuit* of success, the attempts and the eventualities of failure. In the end, Homans and Blau picture man in overly-mechanized terms that allow him little leeway for being human. Such rationalistic models as they offer emphasize goal-attainment and decision-making over alternative means as the primary aspects of social action, and pay minimal attention to the vast undercurrent of communicational and meaning-endowing scramblings of actors. Actors, that is, who perceive their conditions as variously threatening to the successful completion of their projects, and whose activity would better be seen as attempts at "managing" rather than success at completions.

I propose a major break with these dominant traditions in social exchange theory. Our choice of primary exemplar by-passes both Homans with his biological and psychological reductionism and Blau with his economic reductionism. Instead we begin with Marcel Mauss' *The Gift*.[2] First published in 1925, *The Gift* is a comparative study of exchange behavior in various archaic cultures. Mauss' central points concerning social exchange are (1) that it represents a phenomenon "familiar to every known society" contains "moral" features and suggests "one of the bases of social life";[3] (2) that it "fails to conform to the principles of so-called natural economy or utilitarianism,"[4] rather, it is "part of a wide and enduring contract";[5] (3) that it is a behavior characteristic *not* of the relations between individuals but of the relations between groups (individuals as such do not figure in exchange behavior, rather it involves the contractual relations between "moral persons");[6] (4) that members of society exhibit a collective unconsciousness such that they do not ordinarily apprehend these structural and moral underpinnings to their interactive lives.

Mauss' objective is clear. He seeks the mechanism, the bond that sustains the social order. Although he deals in exchange behavior, he is not an exchange theorist; rather he is a morality theorist who sees the particular structure and morality of social exchange as indexically linked with the social order such that the order gives rise to exchange processes and is in turn maintained by these processes. Exchange behaviors (be they market-place economic or social/moral) are not "voluntary, disinterested and spontaneous, but are in fact obligatory and interested."[7] They do not spring from need-pursuit or self-interest; rather they identify a group-integration motive which serves as an order-creating and order-sustaining bond.[8] Exchange is for Mauss what religion is for Durkheim—that is, the producer, carrier and indicator of the moral bond that informs much of social behavior and thus helps hold society together.[9] However, Mauss extends Durkheim in assigning an ontological status to morality as a social fact. It is not to be treated only in a Durkheimian sense *as if* it were real, but as the "institution" of exchange in *real* settings—with a *real* externality and *real* constraining capabilities. Morality appears both as it is institutionally determined and as an invariant property of men's minds. Furthermore, these two exist in a relationship of reflexivity such that one creates the existence of and is in turn sustained by the other.

On the other hand, the social exchange theories of Homans and Blau remove morality from exchange. In its place is substituted respectively biological/psychological and economic utilitarianism.[10] The consequence of this removal is to leave social exchange subject to the whims of supposed rationalities of motives of self-interest; here we have repeatedly argued against this conception of man.

The simple solution then would appear to involve a wholesale acceptance of Mauss' "morality" as the sought after social bond. Simple as this may be, it is also unacceptable. For one thing, "morality" smacks of a metaphysical imprecision of the type that sociology since the time of Comte has attempted to escape. Quite basically it is an empirically indefensible conception as it appears in classical literature. Yet to discard it (as Homans does, for example) is equally unsatisfactory—for it points to bonding more "solid" than the ad hoc quality of utilitarian rationalities.[11] The alternative that I propose is conciliatory to both of these. While we will not pursue "morality" as such, we will seek properties suggestive of a bonding quality no less pervasive (perhaps even more so), yet, properties identifiable empirically as "real." Our aim then is to identify a property or class of properties that exist as invariants on each of two levels: first, as they are reflected in or represented by the institutionalized dictates of social contexts and actors' adaptations to these dictates; and second, on the level at which they figure as more general constituent features in the everyday activity—construction of actors. For the first of these we will draw from Goffman's dramaturgy and for the second from the contributions of Garfinkel's ethnomethodology.

Goffman's sociology consists, of two parts, as we have previously noted. First is a detailed account of the "work" of interaction, the emergence of and maintenance of self, and of the unique and subtle social processes in which these occur. Second is a structural sociology that attempts a depiction of the determination of place and situation over actors' projects and actors' confrontation with these structural, institutionalized aspects of society. We now suggest that these two lines in Goffman have a mutual meeting place, that is, as a resolution of the first part of our search for invariants. Our contention is that there appears in Goffman's sociology a "morality" like that noted by Mauss as: (1) "familiar to every known society"; (2) "part of a wide and enduring contract"; (3) occurring between "moral persons" as opposed to role-less and status-less individuals, and (4) ordinarily not apprehended by actors as moral underpinnings to their interactive lives. This morality we have previously noted as an *exchange of mutually self-supporting conspiracies:* that is, protective practices in which actors conspire to exchange with one another whatever suspension of doubt and disbelief, whatever discretions and tact are deemed necessary to shore up the situation, the act, so as to preserve its sanctity as a spiritual fountain from which they mutually nourish and sustain self-conceptions. Such an exchange ordinarily transcends the give-and-take of most interactive contexts and occurs usually in spite of the potential for mutually exclusive pursuits of self-interest or need-fulfillment.

We see then that Goffman offers an important corrective to exchange theory. His portrayal of interaction as an exchange of mutually self-supporting conspiracies born of the need to counter the precarious conditions inherent in self-defining and self-supporting interactions acts as a buffering agent that makes the rationalistic pill of need-based or self-interest-based exchange theories easier to swallow. Man is less to be seen as the cold, calculating, in-charge functionary of instrumental action, and more to be seen as a threatened, confused, often confined, seeker-of-a-way-out; an inmate, that is, imprisoned in interactional contexts which constantly threaten him with the imposition of their own version of reality, be it the derision of those witness to his gaffes, the spying of those seeking dramatistic advantage over him, or the institutional labeling he must survive. If he is to preserve some sense of self, he is best advised to effect a stance of functional paranoia, for only if he sees the threat of discovery and disclosure in all interactional contexts can he ever hope to be prepared in his act. The essential irony of Goffman's portrait of the actor is that each one, fearful as he must be in his condition, is ordinarily quite willing to suspend his option to challenge the legitimacy of the acts of others. Much like a flock of frightened sheep, each giving way to the inadvertent bumps from others, actors back off, and indeed, willingly exchange cooperative self-supports with others—each of them mindful of the undisturbed flow of the situation from which they mutually derive a sense of calm.

Goffman's contribution to our search for invariant properties is clear. Everyday social life is in many ways to be seen as consisting of features of the "total institution"—among these, in varying degrees, an imposed sequence of activities, a system of formal rulings, an underlying rational plan, a normative orientation which specifies right and wrong, good or bad. These features suggest institutionalized and sub-institutionalized dictates, requiring adaptation on the actor's part. Through the mutuality of subtle and often unique exchange processes, actors conspire to "manage" within these dictates; and, in doing so, they produce and sustain an unspecified sense of social morality. Like Mauss, then, Goffman sees the need for and the existence of a social bond greater than any one actor's self-interest, and pervasive enough to assure each actor of the opportunity to *pursue* self-interest.

Effective as Goffman's corrective to exchange theory may be, it is not yet sufficient to complete a comprehensive theory of social behavior. The major problem with Goffman's work is the "boundedness" imposed by his strict adherence to context and situation. The ploys, tactics, maneuverings of actors in Goffman's encounters, descriptively revealed as they may be by dramaturgical analysis, are only the surface manifestations of an underlying *syntax* or *order* of interaction. Goffman shows us *how* it is done in *some* situations in *some* cultures, but there is a broader, more encompassing "how" that he cannot, given the specificity and cultural boundedness of his treatment, explore. This "how" is the, "How is interaction done?", asked by Garfinkel. While Goffman attends to interactive manifestations in terms primarily responsive to questions of, "*What* are the causes?" and, "*Why* was that action enacted?", Garfinkel's interest is primarily in discovering those *universal* and *invariant properties* of social action which answer the question: "How is interaction *done?*"

Garfinkel's approach is to bracket all considerations of "whys" and "causes" in interaction, and to concentrate on the syntactical nature of interaction insofar as it displays common properties for *all* contexts and situations. This program leads him to view meanings and understandings displayed by members not as elements brought to or imposed upon situations, but as features *constituted* through the situational and practical accomplishments of members.[12] Interaction is seen as a *communication process* in which members *exchange* a sense of meaning and understanding through creative, cooperative and negotiated processes. Like Goffman, Garfinkel views social behavior as essentially problematic, and the actions of individuals as devoted in one way or another to the repair of this precariousness for the sake of their own and others' sense of what-is-going-on-here. Through various practices, members act to insure the factual nature of their own claims and to see and accept others' claims as factual. Interaction is, thus, to be seen as the production and communicative exchange in accountably rational terms of a *sense* of reality. Members in these processes ordinarily display a trust and tacit willingness to accept that which is offered as a to-be-taken-for-granted reality. Doing "accounts" are members' methods and substance for doing meaningful and rationally reportable communications of what is factual and actual.

Garfinkel's search for invariant and universal properties to these communicative processes leads him to suggest the following:

1. Communication ordinarily involves more substantive information than is expressed only in words; such substance is *understood* by members.
2. That which members "understand" is based on certain unspoken features of communication and not on the actual elements of talk.
3. The sequential nature of talk adds to understanding in that

what is first uttered serves to document what comes later in a retrospective-prospective sense.

4. Such underlying meanings and understandings as are seen to exist in communication are tacitly accepted and acknowledged by members. Such tacitly accepted meanings and understandings are reflexively tied to talk insofar as they support talk and are in turn supported by talk.

5. Recognizing the indexical, documentary, and reflexive nature of communication, members ordinarily wait for closures and completions to get a sense of what is going on.

Garfinkel's point is that interaction is to be seen as an exchange of communication; such an exchange displays certain features that are suggested as universal and invariant, and essential for the success of any interaction. Members in this portrayal are depicted as "knowledgeable" regarding these features, yet not on a level that would allow them to "see" their operations. A known-but-not-seen sense prevails in which members do the "work" of such features (formulations, glosses, documentation, etc.), yet ordinarily do not estrange themselves from the process so as to "notice" what actually is happening. In the end, Garfinkel's message is that these features are invariant properties of the communicative work that is interaction, and, indeed, are to be seen as normative.

In his search for the nature of the social bond, then, Garfinkel has left the realm of context and setting (that which is a limitation in Goffman's work). He has sought to transcend the confines of situation and frame, and has pursued instead the underlying, deep structures of invariant procedures. By so doing he has escaped the dilemma of the "awesomeness" of indexicality. That is, how to "understand" in ways not inextricably tied to the specific occasions in which such understanding is made possible.

Garfinkel's work has inspired a whole range of re-evaluations of typical forms of sociological investigations and the types of understanding they typically produce. Central among these re-evaluations is a new perspective on the relationship between individual actors and the dictates of institutionalized contexts. Rather than being based upon the uniqueness and situated character of actors, events and dictates, ethnomethodological studies typically deal in the transsituational, atemporal and universal properties of actors' practices.[13] In so doing, they demonstrate that the actor working within situational dictates typically employs unofficial practices in the completion of tasks and in his general dealings with other actors. These practices are not intended to violate existing rules but are seemingly inevitable meaning-creating and meaning-endowing procedures that make movement and activity possible. Thus, our attention is drawn away from the specifics of institutions and toward the invariant properties of interaction such that these properties will be seen to appear in *all* contexts and at *all* times.

Garfinkel's ethnomethodological concern for invariant properties is seen as the corrective to the incompleteness of Goffman's sociology, and the two may now be acknowledged as having rounded-out the exchange model from its earlier overly-mechanistic and non-institutional forms.

What emerges is a new thesis of social exchange that is seen to account with much more complexity and some entirely new interpretations for the behavior of actors in concert with one another. Such behavior is now believed to be over-simplified when accounted for purely in terms of the rational pursuit of needs-satisfactions or profit. I suggest that any analysis of social exchange cannot be near representative of what is "really going on" unless it is attuned to actors' mutual conspiracies of trust and tact and to underlying invariant processes of meaning-creating and meaning-endowing.

NOTES

1. In addition to the periodic recurrence of "academic" interest in "classic" exchange theory a la Homans, Blau, and the cultural anthropologists (e.g. Mauss, Levi-Strauss, Frazer, and Malinowski), we might note the

occasional "rediscovery" of exchange tenets as the "new and viable" social theory. There is presently among some British sociologists a sense of this rediscovery, for example, Anthony Heath, *Rational Choice and Social Exchange* (London: Cambridge Univ. Press, 1976). It is interesting to note the apparent repatriation of exchange theory by British sociology; it is, after all in Great Britain where its origins are discernible.

An interesting topic, but outside the pervue of this study, is a "sociology of knowledge" perspective on the rise and fall of exchange theory. For instance, where else but in the nation that began the rational revolution of industrialization would we expect to locate origins of a theory of rational behavior? And then, is it not almost to *expect* its appropriation by American sociology? And, why has it figured so lightly in nations where "idealism" has dominated years of social thought? All these types of issues remain unsurveyed, and in need of pursuit.

2. Mauss' work with social exchange has been for the most part under-represented in contemporary literature. Homans and Blau, for example, between them, make a scant half-dozen passing mentions of his contributions. Mauss is most often relegated to the honorific but mostly impotent place of having produced an "anthropological classic."

3. Mauss, *The Gift*, p. 2.

4. Ibid., p. 69.

5. Ibid., p. 3.

6. Ibid. Ekeh (*Social Exchange Theory*, p. 32, n. 1) notes a sociological distinction between "person" and "individual" by citing the claim of Park and Burgess (*Introduction to the Science of Sociology*, Chicago: University of Chicago Press, 1922, p. 5) that "the person is an individual who has a status. We come to this world as individuals. We acquire status, and become persons." Mauss' exclusion of the "individual" from his view of social exchange clearly indicates that he sees the *group* as the basic and elementary unit in these processes.

7. Mauss, *The Gift*, p. 1.

8. Mauss indicates three obligations deriving from exchange processes: to repay gifts received; to give; and to receive (ibid, pp. 10–11). These clearly indicate that group-integration-based and not individual-based motives are involved. For, "to refuse to give, or fail to invite is—like refusing to accept—the equivalent of a declaration of war; it is a refusal of friendship and intercourse." (ibid., pp. 10–11).

9. Like Durkheim, Mauss (ibid., p. 75) argues against utilitarian motives. "The mere pursuit of individual ends is harmful to the ends and peace of the whole...and hence, in the end to the individual." And, like Durkheim, Mauss' work traces exchange processes from their "elementary forms."

10. See for example Homans and Schneider (*Marriage, Authority and Final Causes*). Blau *does* speak of "trust" (*Exchange and Power*, p. 94) however, it is not seen as a reality sui generis, rather it is a property "built up" (ibid., p. 454) only through exchange processes themselves. Similarly, Blau's "fair exchange" and Homans' "distributive justice" are so mitigated by reward pay-offs and economic rationalities that they do not qualify as elements of a pervasive morality. Homans and Blau deal in what Heath (*Rational Choice*, p. 138) calls a "morality of desert" by which people are

given what their acts merit. Mauss would argue that exchange morality is blind to personal merit and exists as an obligatory social contract. "Trust" may be demonstrated and validated by each obligation but otherwise has an existence sui generis.

11. Homans (*Social Behavior*, 1974, p. 218) suggests that Mauss sees a "norm of reciprocity" (a la Gouldner, 1960) in social exchange; however, Homans rejects this conception, claiming that no norm can be self-reinforcing.

12. In ways, Garfinkel's ethnomethodology is reminiscent of a programmatic concern in Mauss' work. In *The Gift*, Mauss indicates his concern with "words and meanings" (p. 2), the symbolic value and quality of gifts and prestations, and most importantly, the *rules* that govern these meanings and values.

13. A typical format for study among many second and third generation ethnomethodologists (many students of Garfinkel) is the structure and concreteness of institutionalized settings. It is here that they can most dramatically illustrate the dominance of invariant properties (e.g., "et cetera," "glossing") over officially prescribed rules for behavior. See, for example: Don H. Zimmerman, "Paper Work and People Work: A Study of a Public Assistance Agency," unpublished doctoral dissertation, Department of Sociology, University of California at Los Angeles, 1966; H. Sacks, "Notes on Police Assessment of Moral Character," in D. Sudnow, (ed.) *Studies in Interaction* (New York: Free Press, 1972); L. Wieder, "The Convict Code: A study of a Moral Order as a Persuasive Activity," unpublished doctoral dissertation, Department of Sociology, University of California at Los Angeles, 1969; Don Zimmerman "Record Keeping and the Intake Process in a Public Welfare Agency," in Stanton Wheeler (ed.), *On Record* (New York: Basic Books, 1970).

References

Abrahamsson, Bengt. "Homans on Exchange: Hedonism Revisited." *American Journal of Sociology* 76 (1970):273–285.

Aron, Raymond. *Main Currents in Sociological Thought.* 2 vols. New York: Basic Books, 1967.

Attewell, Paul. "Ethnomethodology Since Garfinkel." *Theory and Society* 1 (1974):179–210.

Avineri, Shlomo. *The Social and Political Thought of Karl Marx.* Cambridge: Cambridge University Press, 1968.

Berger, Peter L. *Invitation to Sociology.* Garden City, New York: Doubleday, Anchor Books, 1963.

————, ed. *Marxism and Sociology: Views From Eastern Europe.* New York: Appelton-Century-Crofts, 1969.

Berger, Peter L., and Luckmann, Thomas. *The Social Construction of Reality: A Treatise in the Sociology of Knowledge.* Garden City, New York: Doubleday, Anchor Books, 1967.

Blau, Peter M. "Structural Effects." *American Sociological Review* 25 (1960):178–193.

————. *Exchange and Power in Social Life.* New York: John Wiley & Sons, 1964.

————. "Justice in Social Exchange." In *International Encyclopedia of the Social*

Sciences. David L. Sills, ed. New York: MacMillan, The Free Press, 1968: 452-458. Vol. 7.

————. "Objectives of Sociology." In *A Design for Sociology: Scope, Objectives, and Methods.* Robert Bierstedt, ed. Philadelphia: The American Academy of Political and Social Sciences, 1969, pp. 43-71.

Blum, Alan F. "The Corpus of Knowledge as a Normative Order." In *Theoretical Sociology: Perspectives and Developments.* J. McKinney and E. Tiryakian, eds. pp. 319-336.

————. "Theorizing." In *Understanding Everyday Life.* Jack D. Douglas, ed. pp. 305-323.

Burke, Kenneth. *Permanence and Change.* Indianapolis: Bobbs-Merrill, 1935, 1965.

————. *A Grammar of Motives.* Englewood Cliffs, New Jersey: Prentice-Hall, 1945.

————. *A Rhetoric of Motives.* Englewood Cliffs, New Jersey: Prentice-Hall, 1950.

Chomsky, N. *Aspects of a Theory of Syntax.* Cambridge, Massachusetts: M.I.T. Press, 1965.

Cicourel, Aaron. *Methods and Measurement in Sociology.* New York: The Free Press, 1964.

————. "The Acquisition of Social Structure: Toward a Developmental Sociology of Language and Meaning." In *Understanding Everyday Life.* Jack D. Douglas, ed. pp. 136-168.

————. "Basic and Normative Rules in the Negotiation of Status and Role." *Recent Sociology No. 2.* In Hans P. Dreitzel, ed. Pp. 4-45.

————. "Cross Modal Communication: The Representational Context of Sociolinguistic Information Processing." *Monograph Series on Language and Linguistics* No. 25. Georgetown School of Language and Linguistics, 1970.

————. *Cognitive Sociology: Language and Meaning in Social Interaction.* New York: The Free Press, 1974.

Cohen, Jere. "Moral Freedom Through Understanding in Durkheim." *American Sociological Review* 40 (1975):104-106.

Coser, Lewis. "Presidential Address: Two Methods in Search of a Substance." *American Sociological Review* 40 (December 1975):691-700.

Costner, H. L., and Leik, R. K. "Deductions from Axiomatic Theory." *American Sociological Review* 29 (December 1964):819-835.

Denisoff, S., Callahan, O., and Levine, M. *Theories and Paradigms in Contemporary Sociology.* Itasca, Illinois: F. E. Peacock Publishers, 1974.

Denzin, Norman K. "Symbolic Interactionism and Ethnomethodology." In *Understanding Everyday Life.* Jack D. Douglas, ed. Pp. 261-286.

Deutsch, Morton. "Homans in the Skinner Box." *Sociological Inquiry* 34 (1964): 156-165.

Dilthey, Wilhelm. "On the Special Character of the Human Sciences." In *Verstehen: Subjective Understanding in the Social Sciences.* Marcello Truzzi, ed.

Douglas, Jack D. *Understanding Everyday Life*. Chicago: Aldine Publishing Co., 1970.

Dreitzel, Hans Peter, ed. *Recent Sociology No. 2*. New York: Macmillan, 1970.

Durkheim, Emile. *The Elementary Forms of The Religious Life*. Translated by Joseph Ward Swain. New York: The Free Press, 1968.

—————. *Suicide*. J. A. Spaulding and G. Simpson, trans. New York: The Free Press of Glencoe, 1951.

—————. *Education and Sociology*. New York: The Free Press, 1956.

—————. *The Division of Labor in Society*. New York: The Free Press, 1964.

—————. *The Rules of Sociological Method*. New York: The Free Press, 1966.

Ekeh, Peter P. *Social Exchange Theory: The Two Traditions*. Cambridge, Mass.: Harvard University Press, 1974.

Emmerson, Richard M. "Operant Psychology and Exchange Theory." In *Behavioral Sociology*. Robert L. Burgess and Don Bushwell, Jr., eds. New York: Columbia University Press, 1969, pp. 379-405.

—————. "Exchange Networks and Groups as Exchange Systems." In Joseph Berger, Morris Zelditch, and Bo Anderson, eds. *Sociological Theories in Progress*. Vol. II. Boston: Houghton-Mifflin, 1972.

Frazer, Sir James G. *Totemism and Exogamy: A Treatise on Certain Early Forms of Superstition and Society*. London: Dawsons of Pall Mall, 1910, 1968.

Garfinkel, Harold. "Perception of the Other." Unpublished Ph.D. dissertation. Harvard University, 1952.

—————. "Conditions of Successful Degredation Ceremonies." *American Journal of Sociology* 61 (1956):420-424.

—————. "Some Sociological Concepts of Methods for Psychiatrists." *Psychiatric Research Reports* 6 (1956):181-195.

—————. "Aspects of the Problem of Common Sense Knowledge of Social Structures." *Transactions of the Fourth World Congress of Sociology*. Vol. 4. Milan: Stressa, 1959, pp. 51-65.

—————. "Common-Sense Knowledge of Social Structures: The Documentary Method of Interpretation." In *Theories of the Mind*. J. M. Scher, ed. New York: Free Press, 1962, pp. 689-712.

—————. "A Conception of, and Experiments with, 'Trust' as a Condition of Stable Concerted Actions." In *Motivation and Social Interaction*. O. J. Harvey, ed. New York: Ronald Press, 1963, pp. 187-238.

—————. *Studies in Ethnomethodology*. Englewood Cliffs, New Jersey: Prentice-Hall, 1967.

—————. "Practical Sociological Reasoning: Some Features in the Work of the Los Angeles Suicide Prevention Center." In *Essays in Self-Destruction*. E. S. Shneidman, ed. New York: Science House, 1967, pp. 171-187.

Garfinkel, Harold, and Sacks, Harvey. "On Formal Structures of Practical Actions." In J. C. McKinney and E. A. Tiryakian, eds. *Theoretical Sociology: Perspectives and Developments*.

Gerth, H. H., and Mills, C. W. *From Max Weber: Essays in Sociology*. New York: Oxford University Press, 1958.

Glaser, Barney, and Strauss, Anselm. *The Discovery of Grounded Theory*. Chicago: Aldine Publishing Co., 1967.

Goffman, Erving. "On Cooling the Mark Out." *Psychiatry* 15 (1952):451-63.

————. "Communication and Conduct in an Island Community." Unpublished Doctoral Dissertation: Department of Sociology, The University of Chicago, 1953.

————. "On Face Work: An Analysis of Ritual Elements in Social Interaction." *Psychiatry* 18 (1955):213-31.

————. "Where the Action Is." In *Interaction Ritual*. Pp. 149-270.

————. "Embarassment and Social Organization." *American Journal of Sociology* 62 (1956):264-71.

————. "The Nature of Deference and Demeanor." *American Anthropologist* 58 (June 1956):473-502.

————. "Alienation from Interaction." *Human Relations* 10 (1957):47-60.

————. *The Presentation of Self in Everyday Life*. Garden City, New York: Doubleday Anchor Books, 1959.

————. *Encounters*. Indianapolis, Indiana: The Bobbs-Merrill Co., Inc., 1961.

————. "Mental Symptoms and Public Order." In *Interaction Ritual*.

————. *Asylums*. Carden City, New York: Anchor Books, 1961.

————. *Behavior in Public Places*. New York: The Free Press, 1963.

————. *Stigma: Notes on the Management of Spoiled Identity*. Englewood Cliffs, New Jersey: Prentice Hall, 1963.

————. "The Neglected Situation." In *The Ethnography of Communication*. J. Gumperz and D. Hymes, ed. *American Anthropologist* 66, part 2, 1964.

————. *Interaction Ritual*. Chicago: Aldine Publishing Co., 1967.

————. *Strategic Interaction*. New York: Ballantine Books, 1969.

————. *Relations in Public*. New York: Harper & Row, 1972.

————. *Frame Analysis: An Essay on the Organization of Experience*. Cambridge, Mass.: Harvard University Press, 1974.

Gouldner, Alvin W. "The Norm of Reciprocity: A Preliminary Statement." *American Sociological Review* 25 (1960):161-179.

————. *The Coming Crisis of Western Sociology*. New York: Avon Books, 1970.

Habermas, Jürgen. *Knowledge and Human Interests*. Boston: Beacon Press, 1971.

————. "Some Distinctions in Universal Pragmatics." *Theory and Society* 3, 1976.

Hall, Calvin S., and Lindzey, Gardner. *Theories of Personality*. New York: John Wiley and Sons, Inc., 1957.

Heath, Anthony. *Rational Choice and Social Exchange*. London: Cambridge University Press, 1976.

Henderson, Lawrence J. *Pareto's General Sociology: A Physiologist's Interpretation*. New York: Russell & Russell, 1935.

Hiz, Henry. "Kotorbinski's Praxeology." *Philosophy and Phenomenological Research*. (December 1954):238-243.

Homans, George C. *English Villagers of the Thirteenth Century*. New York: Russell and Russell, 1941.

————. *The Human Group*. New York: Harcourt, Brace & World, 1950.

————. "Social Behavior as Exchange." *American Journal of Sociology* 63 (May 1958):597-606.

————. *Social Behavior: Its Elementary Forms*. New York: Harcourt, Brace & World, 1961. Revised edition 1974.

————. *Sentiments and Activities*. New York: The Free Press, 1962.

————. "Bringing Men Back In." *American Sociological Review* 29 (1964):809-818.

————. "Fundamental Social Processes." In *Sociology*. Neil J. Smelser, ed. New York: Wiley and Sons, 1967.

————. "A Life of Synthesis." *American Behavioral Scientist* 12 (1968).

————. "The Sociological Relevance of Behaviorism." In *Behavioral Sociology*. Robert L. Burgess and Don Bushwell, eds. New York: Columbia University Press, 1969.

Homans, George C. and Curtis, Charles P. *An Introduction to Pareto: His Sociology*. New York: Howard Fertig, 1934, 1970.

Homans, George C. and Schneider, David M. *Marriage, Authority, and Final Causes: A Study of Unilateral Cross-Cousin Marriage*. New York: The Free Press, 1955.

Ichheiser, Gustav. "Misunderstandings in Human Relations: A Study in False Social Relations." Supplement to *The American Journal of Sociology* 55 (September 1949).

Jarvie, I. C. *The Revolution in Anthropology*. London: Routledge & Kegan Paul, 1964.

Kaplan, A. *The Conduct of Inquiry*. San Francisco: Chandler, 1964.

Kaufman, Felix. *Methodology of the Social Sciences*. New York: Oxford University Press, 1944.

Kuhn, Thomas S. *The Structure of Scientific Revolutions*. Chicago: University of Chicago Press, 1962.

Levi-Strauss, Claude. *Les Structures Elementaires de la Parente*. Paris: Presses Universitaires de France, 1949.

Lyman, Stanford M. "Civilization: Contents, Discontents, Malcontents." *Contemporary Sociology* 2 (July 1973):360-366.

————. *The Drama of Social Reality*. New York: Oxford University Press, 1975.

Lyman, Stanford M. and Scott, Marvin B. *A Sociology of the Absurd*. New York: Appleton-Century-Crofts, 1970.

Maddi, Salvatore, and Costa, Paul T. *Humanism in Personology: Alport, Maslow, and Murray*. Chicago: Aldine Atherton, Inc., 1972.

Mannheim, Karl. *Ideology and Utopia*. New York: Harcourt Brace Jovanovich, 1936.

————. "On the Interpretation of Weltenschauung." *Essays on the Sociology of Knowledge*. New York: Oxford University Press, 1952.

Manning, Peter K. "Review of Erving Goffman's *Relations in Public*." *The Sociological Quarterly* 14 (Winter 1973):135-43.

————. "Existential Sociology." *The Sociological Quarterly* 14 (Spring 1973):200-225.

Marx, Karl. *Contribution to the Critique of Political Economy*. London: Lawrence and Wishart, 1971.

———. *Theories of Surplus Value*. London: Lawrence and Wishart, 1972.

———. *Early Writings*. New York: Vintage Books, 1975.

Marx, Karl and Engels, F. *The German Ideology*. New York: International Publishers, 1846, 1947.

Mauss, Marcel. *The Gift: Forms and Functions of Exchange in Archaic Societies*. Ian Cunnison, trans. Glencoe, Illinois: The Free Press, 1954.

McHugh, P. "On the Failure of Positivism." In *Understanding Everyday Life*. Jack D. Douglas, ed. Pp. 324-335.

McKinney, J. and Tiryakian, E., eds. *Theoretical Sociology: Perspectives and Developments*. New York: Appleton-Century-Crofts, 1970.

Mead, George Herbert. *The Philosophy of the Present*. La Salle, Illinois: Open Court Publishing Co., 1932.

———. *The Philosophy of the Act*. Chicago: The University of Chicago Press, 1938.

———. *Mind, Self and Society*. Chicago: University of Chicago Press, 1934.

Mills, C. Wright. *The Sociological Imagination*. New York: Oxford University Press, 1959.

Mulkay, M. J. *Functionalism, Exchange and Theoretical Strategy*. New York: Schocken Books, 1971.

Murray, Henry A. *Explorations in Personality*. New York: Oxford Press, 1938.

Nisbet, Robert. *Emile Durkheim*. Englewood Cliffs, New Jersey: Prentice-Hall, 1956.

———. *The Sociology of Emile Durkheim*. New York: Oxford University Press, 1974.

O'Neill, John. "Self-Prescription and Social Machiavellianism." *Sociology As a Skin Trade*. New York: Harper and Row, 1972, p. 11-19.

Pareto, Vilfredo. *The Mind and Society*. New York: Dover Publications, Inc., 1963.

Park, R. and Burgess, E. *Introduction to the Science of Sociology*. Chicago, Illinois: University of Chicago Press, 1922.

Parsons, Talcott. "Levels of Organization and the Mediation of Social Interaction." *Sociological Inquiry* 34 (1964):207-220.

———. *The Social System*. Glencoe, Illinois: The Free Press, 1951.

———. *The Structure of Social Action*. New York: The Free Press, 1968.

———. "Comment on Pope and Cohen." *American Sociological Review* 40 (1975):106-111.

Pope, Whitney. "Classic on Classic: Parson's Interpretation of Durkheim." *American Sociological Review* 38 (1973):399-415.

Sacks, Harvey. "Sociological Description." *Berkely Journal of Sociology* 8 (1963):1-17.

Sartre, Jean Paul. "No Exit." The English Version by Stuart Gilbert. New York: Knopf, 1946.

Schroyer, Trent. "Toward a Critical Theory for Advanced Industrial Society." In *Recent Sociology No. 2*. Hans P. Dreitzel, ed.

182

Schutz, Alfred. "Phenomenology and the Social Sciences." In Marvin Farber, ed. *Philosophical Essays in Memory of Edmund Husserl*. Cambridge, Mass.: Harvard University Press, 1940, p. 164-186.

————. "Some Leading Concepts in Phenomenology." *Social Research* 12 (1945):77-79.

————. "On Multiple Realities." *Philosophical and Phenomenological Research* 4 (1945):533-575.

————. "Choosing Among Projects of Action." *Philosophical and Phenomenological Research* 12 (1951):161-184.

————. "Common Sense and Scientific Interpretation of Human Action." *Philosophical and Phenomenological Research* 14 (1953):1-37.

————. *Collected Papers I: The Problem of Social Reality*. Maurice Natanson, ed. The Hague: Martinus Nijhoff, 1962.

————. *Collected Papers II: Studies in Social Theory*. Arvid Broderson, ed. The Hague: Martinus Nijhoff, 1964.

————. *Collected Papers III: Studies in Phenomenological Philosophy*. I. Schutz, ed. The Hague: Martinus Nijhoff, 1966.

————. *The Phenomenology of the Social World*. George Walsh and Frederick Lehnert, trans. Evanston, Illinois: Northwestern University Press, 1967.

Secord, P. F., and Backman, C. W. *Social Psychology*. New York: McGraw-Hill, 1964.

Simmel, Georg. *The Sociology of Georg Simmel*. Translated and edited by Kurt H. Wolff. New York: The Free Press, 1950.

————. *Conflict and the Web of Group-Affiliations*. New York: The Free Press, 1955.

Skinner, B. F. *The Behavior of Organisms*. New York: Appleton-Century-Crofts, 1938.

————. *Science and Human Behavior*. New York: Macmillan, 1953.

Spencer, Herbert. *The Principles of Sociology*. New York and London: Appleton and Company, 1893.

————. *Social Statics*. London: Chapman, 1951.

Staats, Arthur. "Skinnerian Behaviorism: Social Behaviorism or Radical Behaviorism." *The American Sociologist* 11 (February 1976):59-60.

Sudnow, D., ed. *Studies in Interaction*. New York: The Free Press, 1972.

Swingewood, Alan. *Marx and Modern Social Theory*. New York: John Wiley and Sons, 1975.

Thibaut, J. W., and Kelley, H. H. *The Social Psychology of Groups*. New York: Wiley, 1959.

Tiryakian, Edward. "Existential Phenomenology and the Sociological Tradition." *American Sociological Review* 30, vol. 5 (October 1965).

Truzzi, Marcello. *Verstehen: Subjective Understanding in the Social Sciences*. Reading, Mass.: Addison-Wesley Pub. Co., 1974.

Urbanek, Edward. "Roles, Masks and Characters: A Contribution to Marx's Idea of the Social Role." In *Marxism and Sociology: Views from Eastern Europe*. Peter L. Berger, ed.

Veblen, Thorstein. "The Intellectual Pre-Eminence of Jews in Modern Europe." *Political Science Quarterly* (March 1919).

Weber, Max. *Economy and Society.* 3 vols. New York: Bedminister Press, 1968.

Wheeler, Stanton, ed. *On Record.* New York: Basic Books, 1970.

Wieder, Lawrence D. "The Convict Code: A Study of a Moral Order as a Persuasive Activity." Unpublished Doctoral Dissertation: Department of Sociology. University of California at Los Angeles, 1969.

Wilson, Thomas P. "Normative and Interpretive Paradigms in Sociology." In *Understanding Everyday Life.* Jack D. Douglas, ed. Pp. 57-79.

Wrong, Dennis. "The Oversocialized Conception of Man in Modern Sociology." *The American Sociological Review* 26 (April 1961).

Young, T. R. "The Politics of Sociology: Gouldner, Goffman and Garfinkel." In Denissof, Callahan and Levine, eds. *Theories and Paradigms in Contemporary Sociology.* Itasca, Illinois: Peacock, 1974, pp. 431-41.

Zetterberg, Hans L. *On Theory and Verification in Sociology.* Stockholm: Almquist and Wiksell, 1954. Revised edition. Totowa, New Jersey: The Bedminster Press, 1963.

Zimmerman, Don. "Paper Work and People Work: A study of a Public Assistance Agency." Unpublished Doctoral Dissertation: Department of Sociology, University of California at Los Angeles, 1966.

———. "Record Keeping and the Intake Process in a Public Welfare Agency." In *On Record.* Wheeler, ed.

Zimmerman, Don, and Pollner, Marvin. "The Everyday World as a Phenomenon." In *Understanding Everyday Life.* Jack D. Douglas, ed. pp. 80-103.

Index

186

Murray, Henry A., 16–18, 29, 32–33, 40–41

O

Order, 105

P

Pareto, Vilfredo, 12–18, 29–32, 40
Parsons, Talcott, 43, 74, 139
Pollner, Marvin, 132
Power, 47–48, 60–66, 73–78, 135–136
"Protective Practices," 109

S

Sacks, Harvey, 132
Schneider, David M., 19–21, 41
Schutz, Alfred, 141, 145

Self, 112–113, 115
Self-interest, 57–60, 75
Simmel, Georg, 38
Skinner, B. F., 21–22, 34–35, 41–42
Smith, Adam, 19
Spencer, Herbert, 19

T

"Tact," 109–110
"Total institutions," 117–120
Trust, 66–67, 75

U

Urbanek, Edward, 86
Utilitarianism, 19

Z

Zimmerman, Don, 132